One Hundred Things to do at Universal Studios Orlando Before You Die

The Ultimate Bucket List – Universal Studios Florida and Universal's Islands of Adventure Edition

CATHERINE F. OLEN

One Hundred Things to do at Universal Orlando Before you Die
The Ultimate Bucket List – Universal Studios Florida and Universal's Islands of Adventure Edition

© 2020 Catherine Olen

All Rights Reserved. No portion of this book may be reproduced, stored in a retrieval system, or transmitted in any form or by any means – electronic, mechanical, photocopy, recording, scanning or other – except for brief quotations in critical reviews or articles, without the prior written permission of the publisher. Subject to permission under section 107 and/or 108 of the 1976 United States Copyright act. Permission requests should be addressed to the publisher wwww.mousehangover.com. 949-234-7332

First paperback edition August 2020
ISBN 978-1-64822-010-4 (paperback)
ISBN 978-1-64822-011-1 (eBook)

Published by Mouse Hangover
www.Mousehangover.com

Please note: Every effort has been made to ensure the accuracy of the information throughout this book. The information is believed to be accurate at the time of printing. The publisher and author are not responsible for errors or omissions for changes to details or the consequences of the reader's reliance on the information provided.
Attraction closures or updates are not the responsibility of the publisher or author and cannot be guaranteed at the time of use of this book.

Readers are welcome to contact the publisher for comments, updates, or questions.

Disclaimer

Several Universal enthusiasts have verified all of the information found in this book, but I am aware that the décor of Universal Studios changes regularly. If there are changes, you can visit www.MouseHangover.com for current updates. If you have come across a change before me, please email me so the changes can be noted.

I hope you find your way through the Universal Studios theme park with new eyes and enjoy your hunt for the details every guest can experience.

Note: All content is subject to change without notice. Ride closures, construction, or overlays for the Halloween and Christmas holidays may alter the content temporarily due to park-wide decorations.

This book uses Universal Studios copy-righted characters, registered trademarks, marks, and registered marks of NBC Universal. J.K. Rowling copyrighted characters, registered trademarks, marks, and registered marks. Living Books owned characters, including Dr. Seuss's characters, registered trademarks, marks, and registered marks. Disney owned characters, registered trademarks,

marks, and registered marks. The Simpsons, a registered trademark of 20th Century Fox created by Matt Groening.

All reference to celebrity names, trademarks, marks, and registers marks are the property of the governing body; Mousehangover.com is in no way affiliated with these entities.

All references to these properties are made solely for editorial purposes. Neither the author nor the publisher makes any commercial claim to their use, and neither is affiliated with Universal Studios or NBC in any way.

About the Author

Catherine Olen has been visiting Universal Studios theme parks since she was a small child. Olen fell in love with the parks built through the imagination of founder Carl Laemmle and became an annual pass holder in 1991 and has held an annual pass ever since.

Olen first traveled to Universal Studios Orlando at the age of thirty, immediately falling in love with the Florida parks. She has traveled to the Universal Studios Orlando theme parks each year since and now travels to Orlando several times a year to revel in the new attractions as well as the classic favorites.

Olen now shares her love of all things Universal in *One Hundred Things to do at Universal Orlando Before you Die.*

Come Check Us Out

Check out new books, video, and news at
www.Mousehangover.com
Subscribe to Mouse Hangover
Instagram - @TheMouseHangover
Twitter - @Mousehangover
Facebook - @Mousehangover
@WDWScavengerHunt

YouTube – Mouse Hangover

Other books:

One Hundred Things to do at Disneyland Before you Die
One Hundred Things to do at Walt Disney World Before you Die
One Hundred Things to do at Universal Studios Hollywood Before you Die
The Great Disneyland Scavenger Hunt
The Great Walt Disney World Scavenger Hunt
The Great Universal Orlando Scavenger Hunt
The Great Universal Studios Hollywood Scavenger Hunt

Dedication

This book is dedicated to the millions of people who find Magic and Wonder within the gates of Universal Orlando.

To Carl Laemmle, the dreamer who created one of the first movie studios in Hollywood.

To everyone whose unconditional love and support made this journey possible, I love you all!

Table of Contents

Introduction xiii

Before you Enter the Parks 1

Universal Studios Florida 7

   Production Central 8
      Shrek 4-D 10
      Despicable Me Minion Mayhem 12
      Universal Studios' Classic Monster Café 15
      Rip Ride Rockit 16
      Transformers™: The Ride 3D 17

   New York 19
      Race Through New York Starring
      Jimmy Fallon™ 19
      Revenge of the Mummy 24

   San Francisco 29
      Fast & Furious: Supercharged™ 33

   The Wizarding World of Harry Potter™ -
   Diagon Alley™ 41
      Weasley's Wizard Wheezes 48
      Gladrags Wizardwear™ 49
      Ollivanders™ 53
      Harry Potter and the Escape from Gringotts™ 54
      Knockturn Alley™ 58

  Borgin and Burkes™ 59

World Expo 71
  Men in Black™: Alien Attack 72

Springfield: Home of the Simpsons 75
  The Simpsons Ride™ 76
  Duff Brewery 78
  The Kwik-E-Mart 79
  Moe's Tavern 82

Central Park 85

Woody Woodpecker's KidZone 87
  The E.T. Adventure 89
  Fievel's Playland 90
  A Day in the Park with Barney 90
  Curious George Goes to Town 91

Hollywood 93
  Universal Horror Makeup Show 94

Islands of Adventure 100

Introduction 101

Port of Entry™ 103

Marvel Superhero Island® 110
  The Incredible Hulk Coaster™ 110
  Doctor Doom's Fearfall® 113
  The Amazing Adventures of Spider-man® 116

Toon Lagoon™ 122
  Popeye & Bluto's Bilge-rat Barges 130
  Dudley Do-Right's Ripsaw Falls® 134

Skull Island: Reign of Kong 137

Jurassic Park 140

The Wizarding World of Harry Potter™ -
Hogsmeade™ 146
    Harry Potter and the Forbidden Journey™ 147
    Flight of the Hippogriff™ 153
    Ollivanders™ 155
    The Owl Post™ 157
    Dervish and Banges™ 158
    Gladrags Wizardwear™ 159
    Hogs Head™ 160
    The Three Broomsticks™ 161
    Honeydukes™ 162
    Hagrid's Magical Creatures
    Motorbike Adventure™ 163

The Lost Continent 167

Seuss Landing™ 173
    The Cat in the Hat™ 181

Introduction

Opening summer of 1990, Universal Studios Florida brought the experience of the movies to guests walking through the gates of this brand-new theme park. While Universal films have thrilled audiences for more than one hundred years, the theme park brought a new platform to put guests right in the middle of the action with attractions like the Jurassic Park River Adventure and Men in Black: Alien Attack™

The theme park opened with just a few shows like Alfred Hitchcock: The Art of Making Movies and the "Murder She Wrote" Mystery Theater that gave guests an interactive show that demonstrated how these iconic television shows and movies were created.

The Florida theme park included working sound stages where several 1990's television shows were filmed similar to the original Universal Studios in Hollywood, California.

The guests could board a tram for a short tour through the sound stages and theme park where they might see inside open doors for a glimpse into a sound stage and then passing by the prop graveyard, which housed many of the props from current productions and their favorite films. The guests would get a view of the areas of the park that they would walk through later to access the other shows and attractions during this tram tour, but the tour became challenging due to the high volume of guests walking alongside the trams. The tram tour was retired in 1995 to make way for bigger and better attractions.

Some of the first rides guests could experience include the Wacky World of Hanna Barbera and Kongfrontation, both of which would bring guests into the action to make them feel like they were in these popular properties. The Earthquake attraction would round out the thrill rides available to guests at the opening of Universal Studios Florida while trying to make the property more like Hollywood where actual filming of current televisions shows would happen.

As the years went on, Universal would create new rides to stay up to date. Terminator2: 3-D would continue the story of the well-known *Terminator* films with live-action combining with 3-D video to bring the Terminators right in your face.

Another popular show would be created after the *Twister* film starring Helen Hunt and Bill Paxton, thrilled audiences in the theaters. The guests would experience an F5 tornado while watching the scene destroyed right before their eyes.

With the new millennium, the theme park would become more hi-tech with Shrek 4-D and Fear Factor Live, bringing new films and reality television shows to the theme parks. RipRide Rockit, and Revenge of the Mummy gave the theme park high-intensity roller coaster rides that brought throngs of guests through the gates of the park.

In 1999, Universal would expand to include Universal's Island of Adventure™ to create a different theme park experience with more traditional theme park rides coming to exist within the gates.

Marvel™, Jurassic Park, and Dr. Seuss would give guests a variety of rides so everyone in the family would be included in the adventures.

More recently, Universal Studios Florida has brought the world of Harry Potter to the theme parks with authentic attractions like Harry Potter and the Forbidden Journey™ and the Hagrid's Magical Creatures Motorbike Adventure. Guests would get the opportunity to walk through the shops and sip Butterbeer, just like Harry, Hermione, and Ron. Finally, people could walk through Hogwarts™ castle and step right into the thrilling movies based on the books they love.

Whether guests are looking for a thrill or attractions for the whole family, the Universal Orlando resort offers something for everyone.

Now, *One Hundred Things to do at Universal Orlando* gives guests a chance to get the most out of their time in the theme parks.

Before you Enter the Parks

The Universal Orlando Resort offers much more than theme park rides and shows. When you enter the resort, you will be met with restaurants, shops, and entertainment that will enhance your theme park experiences.

Be sure to plan some time to explore the resort offerings for amazing adventures that await you.

☐ Stay at the Surfside Inn and Suites

> Start your vacation by staying at the Surfside Inn and Suites, where you will feel like you are staying right on the water in this surf-themed hotel.
>
> With rooms and suites overlooking the crystal-clear pool, you will have a great view throughout your stay.

- ☐ Stay at Universal's Cabana Bay Beach Resort

    Enjoy this period-style resort that takes guests back to the 1960s. This brightly colored resort offers guests spacious rooms and countless amenities to enhance their vacation.

- ☐ Stay at Universal's Adventura Hotel

    This stylish hotel offers guests modern convenience with proximity to Universal theme parks. This hotel offers great restaurants and lounges for a relaxing evening to recuperate after long days in the parks.

- ☐ Stay at the Hard Rock Hotel

    Stay at the Hard Rock Hotel, where you will be right in the middle of your favorite rock and roll era. This vibrant hotel puts guests right in the middle of the action where you can lay by the pool to see live rock and roll acts in the lounges.

    Be sure to check out the Hard Rock Hotel for your next vacation.

- ☐ Visit the great restaurants at the Universal CityWalk™

    Food for every taste can be found on the Universal CityWalk™. Fusion Sushi and Sake Bar™ brings authentic cuisine while Hot Dog Hall of Fame™

brings your favorite hot dogs with great toppings. For sit down meals, try Bob Marley – A Tribute to Freedom™ or NBC Sports Grill and Brew™ that gives you rest while enjoying a hearty meal.

Whatever you are looking for can be found at the Universal CityWalk™.

- [ ] Experience the Wantilan Luau at Loews Royal Pacific Resort

    Celebrate your vacation with an authentic luau offering Polynesian food while enjoying live music with hula and fire dancers showing off their amazing talents.

    This one of a kind dining experience gives guests an excellent all-inclusive experience, so be sure to book early.

- [ ] Enjoy Musica Della Note

    Each evening, the Loews Portofino Bay Hotel offers guests opera performed live as you enjoy the outdoor lounges and dining area. These talented performers perform classical music, as well as modern music reimagined.

    Head to the Loews Portofino Bay Hotel for an amazing evening of entertainment.

☐ Enjoy a donut from Voodoo Doughnut

> Step into this bright pink store to taste your favorite donuts created in a fun new way. Within Voodoo Doughnut, the donut artisans have creatively created classic donut flavors with fun décor and flavors not seen in other shops.
>
> Step in and get your favorite on your way to the theme parks.

☐ Indulge your sweet tooth at Toothsome Chocolate Emporium

> Inside the Toothsome Chocolate Emporium, you can find your favorite chocolate flavors in creative ways. The Steampunk aesthetic can be found throughout the displays, so select your favorite chocolates to take home.
>
> For guests looking for something different, try an ice cream sundaes, chocolate desserts, or delicious macarons.

☐ Check out your favorite movies at Cinemark™

> The latest movies can be found at Universal Orlando CityWalk™. Relax while you watch the biggest blockbuster films and snack on your favorite theater snacks.

One Hundred Things to do at Walt Disney World Before you Die

☐ See the Blue Man Group show

> The Blue Man Group has come to Universal Orlando Resort to entertain the whole family. These talented performers offer their unique brand of entertainment using music, lights, and a variety of props to dazzling audiences at Universal Studios Orlando nightly.

☐ See a piece of the Berlin Wall at the entrance to the Blue Man Group show

> This amazing piece of history can be found behind the Hard Rock Café and rarely seen by guests unless they are attending one of the shows.
>
> Do not miss this opportunity to see this historic memorial at Universal Orlando Resort.

☐ Watch the Universal Orlando's Cinematic Celebration™

> Each evening, guests gather at the water's edge at Universal Studios Hollywood to see this spectacular water show that combines music, projections, and dancing water to celebrate your favorite movies. See scenes from blockbuster films as well as animated movies you love.
>
> Universal Orlando's Cinematic Celebration is the perfect ending to your day in the theme

park, so make sure to stay for this truly amazing experience.

☐ Attend the Universal Orlando Resort Halloween Horror Nights™

Guests looking for a terrifying evening can get tickets for the Universal Studios Orlando Halloween Horror Nights event, which are held in September and October. Enter at your own risk as ghouls are waiting in the darkness to create terror for those in attendance.

Walkthrough terrifying mazes themed after your favorite horror films or travel the scare zones with scarers waiting to attack.

This event is not for the faint of heart, so be prepared for the Universal Studios Orlando Resort Halloween Horror Nights™.

Universal Studios Florida

Production Central

As you enter Universal Studios Florida, you will find yourself walking among the soundstages that make up the Hollywood movie studios. Inside these soundstages, you become part of the action when the lights dim and put you right in the movies you love. The beginnings of the Hollywood films include the soundstages that were built to give the producers the ability to create any backdrop for the movies that thrilled audiences and now Universal Studios Florida has recreated these soundstages as the backdrop to the attractions based on your favorite films.

Production Central is just the start of your adventure, but the perfect beginning of your day.

☐ Get your picture with the Universal Studios globe

> One of the greatest icons of Universal Studios is the globe that has been introducing your favorite films since 1927. The Universal globe has taken on many variations over the years but has always maintained the earth circled by an airplane or the Universal Studios' name.

Now you can be the star at the entrance to Universal Studios Florida by posing for a selfie or posing with your family for a memorable photo.

☐ Get your picture on the red carpet

Be treated like a star on the red carpet as you walk through the gates of Universal Studios, Florida. Early each morning, you will see the cast set up for your photoshoot on the red carpet. This is a great memento of your time at the theme park, so take a few moments to get this photo as your first memento of Universal Orlando.

☐ Visit On Location for all your theme park needs

On Location, found just inside the gates of Universal Studios, Florida offers everything you could need for a day in the theme parks.

Whether you need suntan lotions, sunglasses, hats, or sundry items, On Location is a one-stop-shop for all your needs.

☐ Stop at Studio Sweets for something sweet

Studios Sweets offer the best candies and pastries anywhere at the resort. Stop in for your favorite cupcakes, candies, suckers or fudge inside Universal Studios Florida

- [ ] Visit the Universal Studios Store for every souvenir you could dream of

    The Universal Studios Store offers everything you could want in one shop. Inside, you will find clothing, plush toys, collectibles, and wands, along with a wide variety of collectibles.

    Throughout the year, you will find event items from the Universal Halloween Haunt, and great Christmas décor, so stop in to see what your next favorite item will be.

- [ ] Grab a snack at the Today

    The Today show jumped off the television screen and into Universal Studios Florida, as you step through the doors. The Today logo, along with the bright orange set is the backdrop where you can find delicious pastries and coffees to get your day started.

Shrek 4-D

- [ ] Read the newspaper in Shrek 4-D queue

    Throughout the queue for Shrek 4-D, you will find little nods to the land where fairy tale creatures live. Spend some time reading the Medieval Times while you are waiting for your attraction to begin. Catch up on the trial of the dragon or find out why the three bears are angry.

Make sure to read the lead story on the return of Lord Farquaad returning from the grave.

☐ Read the ads in the queue for Shrek 4-D

Find out what is happening in the land of fairy tale creatures when you read the advertisements pinned to the bulletin board outside of Shrek 4-D.

Read about the specials at Foes or the fairy tale creatures' support group meeting. Do not miss some of the personal ads before you are through reading this enchanting newspaper.

☐ Experience the Shrek 4-D attraction

Enter the dungeon of Lord Farquaad and learn about what happened to Shrek and Fiona after they lived happily ever after.

Has Lord Farquaad come back from the grave? Will Shrek and Donkey have to save the princess once more? Will Donkey and Dragon come together to help Shrek on his quest?

Join the action in Shrek 4-D as you come along for the fun.

☐ Find the magic mirror and watch it change

> After your adventure in Shrek 4-D, stop in at the Shrek's Ye Olde Souvenir Shoppe and find the magic mirror behind the counter. If you watch carefully, the mirror will come to life and show the face within.

☐ Examine the map of the fairy tale world

> On one wall inside Shrek's Ye Olde Souvenir Shoppe, you will find a mural size map of the fairy tale world.
>
> This fun map shows guests where Shrek and Donkey had their adventures in the series of films. Now you can see for yourself all of the areas made famous in these films.

Despicable Me Minion Mayhem

☐ Walkthrough Gru's house at Despicable Me Minion Mayhem

> Walk into Gru's home, and you will find a treasure trove of the unusual. Stand in the main room and find the family tree showing all of the oddballs in Gru's family.

Gru's daughters have been working hard decorating the walls while Gru's childhood artwork shows are displayed to show that his plan to steal the moon was planned from his earliest years.

The rhino chair and iron maiden stand high above while the lion head holds the dog, cat, and mouse within its jaws is displayed above the front door.

Be sure to spend some time exploring this truly unusual house before beginning your minion training.

☐ Go through minion training at Despicable Me Minion Mayhem

Being your minion training with an interview with Gru himself before being transformed into a minion and starting your rigorous training.

Navigate the obstacle course and work together with your other minions as you try to complete the various challenges around you. Be careful, or you may have to help Gru save his girls from certain death before you are through.

Be sure to get your groove on at the dance party as you exit this attraction and see yourself on the big screen.

- [ ] Meet Gru, Margo, Edith and Agnes

    Gru and his family are waiting to meet you at the Despicable Me Dance Party on the street outside Despicable Me Minion Mayhem. Stop by and get your picture and autographs with this villain turned good guy and his beautiful daughters.

- [ ] Find your minion gear at Super Silly Stuff

    Once your minion training is complete, you can show off your new status with great souvenirs from Super Silly Stuff. Whether you are looking for clothing, toys, or sweets, Super Silly Stuff has everything a new minion could ask for.

- [ ] Cross the street at the Minion crossing

    At Universal Studios Florida, guests can cross the street at a unique crosswalk. Just outside Super Silly Stuff, you will find a minion crosswalk to add a bit of fun to your day at Universal Studios Florida.

- [ ] See a concert at the Universal Music Plaza Stage

    Throughout the year, guests can see their favorite musical groups perform on the Universal Music Stage Plaza. This open area offers fantastic opportunities to hear live music from the hottest groups in the music scene today.

Be sure to look at the schedule of events to plan your next live concert at Universal Studios Florida.

Universal Studios' Classic Monster Café

☐ Get your picture taken in the electric chair in front of Universal Studios' Classic Monsters Café

> Outside the Universal Studios' Classic Monster Café, guests will find a chair like no other in the theme parks. This replica electric chair offers guests a very unusual picture opportunity, so do not miss this chance to sit in a real movie prop before enjoying a delicious meal at the café.

☐ Check out the horror film memorabilia inside Universal Studios' Classic Monsters Café

> Universal Studios is synonymous with movie monsters. The greatest monster films of all time came from Universal Studios in Hollywood, and now Universal Studios Florida has created an exceptional restaurant experience for you.
>
> Within the Universal Studios' Classic Monster Café, you will have the chance to select dining in many rooms decorated in the fashion of your favorite monster movie. Try Dracula's castle or the Frankenstein lab. Maybe you prefer dining with

the Creature from the Black Lagoon or the Science Fiction dining room. Be sure to explore these fantastically decorated rooms after your meal.

☐ Try an ice-cold drink at Bone Chillin'

Standing just outside the Universal Studios' Classic Monster Café, you will find your favorite movie monsters beckoning you to Bone Chillin' to get an ice-cold slush drink in your favorite flavors. Try Strawberry, Pina Colada, Lemonade or margarita

For guests looking for an adult beverage, try the pina colada or margarita with alcohol or a cold beer.

Rip Ride Rockit

☐ Find the hidden soundtrack on Rip Ride Rockit

Guests riding Rip Ride Rockit will have the chance to select a song to accompany their ride, but few guests know about the secret song list available.

Hold your finger down on the logo at the top of the screen, and you will be able to enter a numeric code for another set of songs. Code 112 offers *Freebird* by Lynyrd Skynyrd, code 304 offer *Its*

Still Rock and Roll to Me by Billy Joel, 122 offers *Start Me Up* by the Rolling Stone, and these are just a few of the options on the secret song list on Rip Ride Rockit.

Transformers™: The Ride 3D

☐ Walkthrough the NEST at Transformers™: The Ride 3D

Your time with the Transformers™ begins as you enter the NEST facility. Enter this top-secret military complex and find where the military has stored the AllSpark, as well as parts of the Decepticons, captured during the battle.

Watch the monitors while working your way through the facility, and you will find out about the mission you are about to embark on. Watch out for Megatron as he is hunting for the Freedom Fighters that are ready to save the planet.

☐ Ride with the Freedom Fighters on Transformers™ the Ride 3D

Optimus Prime needs your help in saving the city from Megatron and his Decepticons. Hop aboard EVAC and help keep the AllSpark from the clutches of Megatron while ensuring you and your fellow Freedom Fighters stay alive.

Travel through the city while a battle rages around you. Keep an eye out for the Decepticons as they take on many different forms. At the end of your mission, Optimus Prime will give you his personal thanks for a mission well done.

☐ Get a picture with Optimus Prime

Optimus Prime is waiting for guests near the NEST facility to get pictures and chat with his new friends. Be sure to have your camera ready to capture this icon of the Transformers™.

☐ Get a picture with Bumblebee

Everyone's favorite Transformer™, Bumblebee, is waiting for guests near the NEST facility. Bumblebee offers his song choices to talk to guests as they get pictures with these great characters from the Transformers™ films.

☐ Get a picture with Megatron

The good guys are not the only Transformers™ waiting for guests at Universal Studios Florida. Megatron is ready to threaten guests and recruit new members of the Decepticons outside the NEST. Keep your guard up as you get pictures with this villain, or you may be his next victim.

New York

Walk through the streets of New York, the most exciting city in the world. From the brownstone buildings to the biggest theaters, you can also experience all of the places that make New York great.

Eat at the restaurants from classic films and watch performers jump right off the screen to sing and dance for you on the street.

Everything from the smallest business to the iconic buildings is right at your feet when you explore New York.

Race Through New York Starring Jimmy Fallon™

☐ Find Bill Paxton's shirt from the movie *Twister*

> Long before Race Through New York with Jimmy Fallon™ came to Universal Studios Florida, this building house the Twister attraction and starred

Bill Paxton, the lead in the film of the same name. Now, guests can find the shirt Paxton wore in this classic film hanging in the front window of this building.

The light blue shirt is worn and wrinkled, showing the wearer used it often.

Be sure to get a picture of this screen worn movie prop.

☐ Find the nods to the Twister attraction

If guests look carefully in the windows at the front of the Race Through New York attraction, you will find several nods to the previous attraction, Twister. Find the Twister Cola advertisement and many other little hints to the previous attraction.

Take some time to examine the window props to see how many hints you can find.

☐ Explore the Tonight Show archives in the lobby of Race Through New York with Jimmy Fallon™

The Tonight Show has a long history on NBC, and the lobby of this attraction is a time capsule to the hosts of this iconic television show.

Guests can find the items that each host used to make this show his own. Johnny Carson and his

Karnac hat, Steve Allen and his sheet music and Conan O'Brien, who hosted this show for one short year.

Be sure to make time to explore these fascinating archives before your boarding group is called.

☐ Join the Rag Time Gals for a performance

On the second floor of the Race Through New York Starring Jimmy Fallon™ attraction, guests will find a small stage where Jimmy Fallon will introduce the Rag Time Gals. This talented group offers a new twister on your favorite songs as they entertain while you are awaiting your race.

This show is a must-see, so be sure to plan your time for this attraction.

☐ Meet Hashtag the Panda

Hashtag, the Panda, is waiting to greet guests with his high energy dancing in the lobby of Race Through New York with Jimmy Fallon™.

Hashtag will pose for pictures with guests after his show if Jimmy has not already worn him out.

☐ Join Jimmy Fallon on Race Through New York with Jimmy Fallon™

> Jimmy Fallon is ready to race you through the street of New York, so get ready for a high-speed chase. See the sights of New York, but be careful, or you may end up in outer space before trying to get back to earth.

☐ Explore the New York facades

> The New York area of Universal Studios Florida offers a glimpse of each area that makes New York the diverse city it has become. From Brownstone street to the theater district, this smaller version gives guests the chance to browse the streets and business facades that make this city iconic.
>
> Spend some time strolling down the streets before your next ride.

☐ Find the Priscilla Hotel from *Thoroughly Modern Millie*

> In the New York section of Universal Studios Florida, guests will find the Priscilla Hotel standing on the corner just off the park. Fans of classic films will recognize this façade from the film *Thoroughly Modern Millie* starring Julie Andrews.

In this film, Andrews rooms here with Mary Tyler Moore as they find love and adventure in this musical film.

Get a selfie with this icon of classic cinema.

☐ See Marilyn Monroe perform

Marilyn Monroe is synonymous with Hollywood, but she is appearing in New York on the street for guests each day.

Arriving in her classic car with her backup dancers, Monroe performers her best-known songs right on the street. This platinum blonde shows off her singing and dancing talent, so be sure to catch her next show.

☐ Have a drink in O'Rourke's Bar and Grill

Fans of the Godfather films may recognize O'Rourke's Bar and Grill from this classic film. Kelly O'Rourke was a tragic character from this film, but O'Rourke's Bar and Grill will give guests a refreshing drink on a hot day.

Inside this New York pub, guests will find Irish memorabilia in every corner and a classic mahogany bar with cold beer and spirits.

Revenge of the Mummy

☐ Check out the artifacts from The Mummy films

> As you enter the Paradise theater and work your way through the queue, guests will come across production storage areas that hold costumes, props, and molds from *The Mummy* series of films.
>
> Look over the bulletin boards to read production notes and scene filming for the next day. These behind the scenes touches bring the film making process to life in Revenge of the Mummy.

☐ Reach out for the key to the book of the dead

> As guests work their way into the tomb of *The Mummy*, you will come across the key to the book of the dead.
>
> Do you dare reach out to make it your own, or will you pass by without succumbing to temptation?

☐ Press your hand to the sarcophagus in the queue for Revenge of the Mummy

> In the center of the lower level of the tomb, guests will walk by the sarcophagus of the mummy. Reach out and place your hand on the top to bring the curse to life.

Do you dare to see what comes of touching the mummy's resting place?

☐ Ride the Mummy rollercoaster

Climb aboard and begin your exploration of the tomb. The film crew warns you not to proceed, but it is too late to turn back. Hold on as the mummy takes control of your fate.

Say a prayer that you come back to civilization alive.

☐ Find the Kitty Kat Club

At the corner of New York street, guests will find the Kitty Kat Club neon sign. For those who have seen the classic musical *Cabaret* starring Liza Minelli, this sign should bring back fond memories.

Cabaret took eight Academy Awards™ at the 1972 awards show and now has been immortalized in New York at Universal Studios Florida.

☐ Watch the Blues Brothers perform

Guests never know which celebrity they may run into on the streets of New York. Now, you have the chance to see the Blues Brothers perform right on the street with their unique brand of talent.

Listen as they bring to life their signature song Soul Man along with many other of your favorite tunes. Do not miss a chance to see this dynamic duo of the silver screen.

☐ Visit the Park Plaza Holiday Shop

Throughout Universal Studios Florida, guests can find souvenirs of every kind but step into the Park Plaza Holiday Shop and find a great souvenir to hang on your Christmas tree.

Ornaments from your favorite films, along with adorable character ornaments can be found in this shop that brings Christmas all year long.

Minions, the Grinch, Harry Potter™, and dozens of others can be found at the Park Plaza Holiday Shop along with wreaths and stockings to decorate your home and remember your time at the theme parks.

☐ Stop at the Palace Theater Arcade for classic video games

The Palace Theater offers guests a great place to go when the heat gets to be too much but also offers classic video games to entertain.

Try your hand at video games themed after your favorite Universal films or try games of skill to collect tickets for unique souvenirs. Traditional claw games give guests a chance to win adorable plush toys or spin the wheel for a chance to get hundreds of tickets.

Whichever your preference, the Palace Theater Arcade has the perfect game for you.

☐ Find the orphanage from *Annie*

Throughout Universal Studios Florida, guests will find facades from their favorite films, and another stands across from the Palace Theater. A bronze plaque for the Hudson Street Home for Girls stands silently on the building, waiting for guests to notice.

This is the very orphanage that little orphan Annie called home before coming to Daddy Warbucks in this famous film.

☐ Grab a bite to eat at Louie's Restaurant

Another nod to the classic film *The Godfather* is Louie's Restaurant in New York. For fans of *The Godfather*, they will remember the iconic scene in which Michael Corleone meets Virgil Sollozzo to end hostilities but kills Sollozzo instead.

For guests looking for a great Italian meal, stop at Louie's during your day for a sit-down meal and rest from the day.

☐ Grab an ice cream at Ben & Jerry's™

> Ben and Jerry's™ has moved into New York to offer guests an ice cream in their favorite flavors. Be sure to indulge your sweet tooth at Ben & Jerry's™ as you stroll through New York.

☐ Grab a caffeinated drink at Starbucks™

> Guests may need a pick me up during their day, and Starbucks™ offers a wide variety of hot and cold drinks and yummy pastries.

Get your favorite on the streets of New York.

San Francisco

Walk along the seaside city by the bay as you find the treasures of San Francisco. Enjoy cocktails or a delicious meal at the water's edge before exploring the iconic buildings known throughout the world.

Whether you are looking for a quiet day or high-speed thrills, you will find everything you could imagine in San Francisco.

☐ Walk through Richter's Burgers

> Richter's Burgers offer hearty meals, but the décor within Richter's will keep you coming back.
>
> Richter's has taken the earthquake to a whole new level with references to the California San Andreas Fault everywhere you look.
>
> From advertisements for earthquake-proof baby carriages to the Lew Wasserman statue on its head, you will not want to miss this quirky and quakey restaurant in San Francisco.

☐ Find Doc Brown from *Back to the Future* within Richter's Burgers

> As you explore Richter's Burgers, you will find a diagram of a seismograph and a picture of the inventor mounted on the wall. Fans of the *Back to the Future* films will recognize this inventor as none other than Doc Brown played by Christopher Lloyd.

☐ Get a picture with the Lew Wasserman statue in San Francisco

> In the center of San Francisco stands the larger than life statue of Lew Wasserman. While most guests may walk by without stopping or noticing this bronze statue, Lew Wasserman was one of the biggest names in Hollywood.
>
> As an agent, Wasserman represented greats like Jimmy Stewart, Bette Davis, and Ronald Reagan. Later, Wasserman would become the head of MCA, the company that purchased Universal Studios.
>
> Wasserman had a career spanning over six decades as a studio executive and talent agent who was instrumental in ending the studio contract system and now has been immortalized at Universal Studios Florida.

☐ Take a picture with Jaws

> Standing at the water's edge, guests will find the shark that terrorized a small community in the 1970's blockbuster *Jaws*. It looks like the fisherman has captured this elusive shark, and now you can get your picture with him near the water in San Francisco.

☐ Pick a pearl at the Pearl Factory

> Another highly unusual souvenir at Universal Studios Florida, is the Pearl Factory on the streets of San Francisco. Guests have the opportunity to select an oyster, and the pearl expert will open and measure your new find for you. Guests can pick their setting on-site or take your new pearl home as it is.

☐ Select something sweet at the San Francisco Pastry Company

> Step through the doors of the San Francisco Pastry Company and find the perfect treat to satisfy your sweet tooth.
>
> Select from handmade cupcakes, candy apples, fudge, and brownies or your favorite candy bar from the shelves packed with sweets for every taste.

Guests can even find souvenirs based on their favorite candies in the San Francisco Pastry Company.

- [ ] Have a sumptuous meal at Lombard's Seafood Grill

    For guests looking for a high-end seafood meal, stop at Lombard's Seafood Grill and find your favorite fresh seafood made daily.

    Select the perfect wine pairing for your meal as you dine by the water of San Francisco.

- [ ] Get a tasty libation at Chez Alcatraz

    Step up to the bar at the water's edge at Chez Alcatraz. Named after the iconic San Francisco prison, Chez Alcatraz, talented bartenders are waiting to pour you your favorite adult beverage on your next visit to Universal Studios Orlando.

- [ ] Find the Ghirardelli façade in San Francisco

    Near the Fast & the Furious: Supercharged™ attraction, guests will find a large red brick building. The Ghirardelli family moved into the building in 1853, making chocolates that would become famous. No tribute to San Francisco would be complete without the Ghirardelli façade.

The San Francisco section now pays homage to this San Francisco landmark.

Fast & Furious: Supercharged™

☐ Find Dom's 1970 Dodge Charger

The black 1970 Dodge Charger Dominic Toretto drove in the *Fast & the Furious* franchise is one of the most iconic picture cars of all time. Now guests can get up close and personal to this famous car.

The vehicles in this series of films are as famous as the actors, and now you can pose for pictures with one of the most recognizable cars in cinematic history.

☐ Find the beer bottle on its side on the picnic table

Throughout the queue for Fast & Furious: Supercharged™ guests will find Easter eggs to the films and actors who have brought these characters to life.

The beer bottle on the picnic table is a nod to the family sitting at the table for meals in the films, but the set decorators at Universal Studios Florida have offered a tribute to actor Paul Walker by tipping on of the bottle on its side.

☐ Walk through the garage and find screen used picture cars

> As you enter the garage area of the queue, guests will notice several racing vehicles in the main room. There are several cars in the queue that fans of the *Fast & Furious* films may see as screen used picture cars.

☐ Find the character names on the black tool chests

> Within the first room of the Fast & Furious: Supercharged™ queue, guests will find large black chests with grey stripes.
>
> In the lower right corner of each, guests will find the name of one of the characters from the films. Lettie, DJ, and Brian are just a few you will find in the main area.

☐ Find a part of Brian's Nissan Skyline in the queue

> While the set decorators could not include every car from the film franchise, they did include a piece of Brains silver and blue Nissan Skyline in the paint shop area of the queue.
>
> Keep an eye out for this tribute as it is in plain sight.

☐ Read the license plates on the wall of the paint shop

> Guests will pass by a workbench with several license plates displayed on the wall and a large red toolbox nearby. If you look very carefully at the side of the toolbox, guests can read the OUTATME plate from *Back to the Future* and the THX 138 plate from *American Graffiti*. Dom's black and gold vanity plate can be found on the wall near this area also.

☐ Find the Beetlejuice bowling pin in the paint shop

> In the area with the license plates on display, guests will find a custom painted bowling pin to the right of the red toolbox. This Beetlejuice bowling pin was not set here by accident; this is another nod to the attraction previously housed in this area. The Beetlejuice Graveyard Revue was retired to bring the new attraction to guests.

☐ Find the Disaster jacket on the chair in the third room of the queue

> As you continue to work your way through the queue, you will come to a third room with the custom truck Tej built. Hanging on a chair near the parts table, you will find a jacket with a Disaster Studios patch on the front.

This is yet another nod to a previous attraction that was housed in this area. The disaster was a special effect show that gave guests a firsthand look at the effects seen in their favorite films.

☐ Find the Beetlejuice figure on the top of the parts desk

Beetlejuice can be found throughout the queue for Fast & Furious: Supercharged™, and now he looks down at you from the top of a part desk with a tall storage area on top.

Keep a keen eye out for this little figure in the third room.

☐ Find the P. Walker footlocker

Tributes to Paul Walker are found throughout the queue, and the footlocker storage area is another. The name P. Walker can be found on the footlocker just past the semi in the third room.

☐ Read the quips on the pictures in the family room

In the family room, you will notice pictures of the stars from the *Fast & the Furious* films. If you look closely, you will notice some of these pictures have a small note attached in a corner or nearby on the bulletin board. These funny quips are little digs the actors have posted for each other. One of the family members even posted a tiny baby oil advertisement near a picture of Dwayne Johnson.

☐ Find the various nods to actor Paul Walker in the family room

> Within the family room, Paul Walker is found in several ways. Whether it is the picture of Walker, the tennis shoes beneath the lockers, Brian's shirt hanging on the locker, or the miniature Nissan Skyline, these items are all very personal to the Brain character played by Paul Walker and the set designers have made his presence felt throughout the queue.

☐ Find the nod to Walt Disney in the war room

> Guests will step into a room with several monitors and a large illuminated map. If guests look at the list of names on one of the monitors, the name Walter Elias is listed. This is the first and middle name of Walt Disney World founder, Walt Disney.

☐ Find Walker St. on the illuminated map

> The map in the war room shows a street map with the names of the streets handwritten.
>
> If you look carefully, Walker St. is seen on this map. This is yet another nod to actor Paul Walker.

☐ Read the wanted posters in the queue

> Throughout the queue, the wanted posters for the bad guy, Owen Shaw, and his gang can be seen. Spend some time reading these wanted posters to see the specific set of skills each member of Owen Shaw's gang has and what previous crimes they are wanted for by the authorities.

☐ Find the electrical boxes near the load area of the queue

> Guests working their way through the queue to the load area will walk by a set of electric boxes that seem to be part of the building. These nondescript boxes are another way for the set designers to offer a mention of the previous attractions housed in this area.
>
> Each of these boxes has an ID with a different number. These IDs coincide with the attractions and the month and year they opened. EQ 06 1990 for Earthquake June 1990, DI 01 2008 for Disaster January 2009 and FF 03 2018 – Fast & Furious: Supercharged™ March 2018.
>
> While the theme park has grown and changed throughout the years, the set designers never forget the previous attractions that have been a part of the history of Universal Studios Florida.

One Hundred Things to do at Walt Disney World Before you Die

☐ Ride with your favorite street racers on Fast & Furious: Supercharged™

> Step aboard a party bus and find yourself face to face with Owen Shaw looking for the witness. Race with your favorite street racers who will protect you like their own family.
>
> Keep your head down as your bus is attacked from every side by the bad guys before your final escape with Dom, Lettie, and Roman helping to keep you and the witness safe.

☐ Find the Jurassic Park sign in the parking garage area of Fast & Furious: Supercharged™

> As you enter the parking garage on your party bus, you will hear the sounds of gunshots outside. Stop for a moment to look around, and you may find the parking level in Jurassic with the profile of a dinosaur on one of the pillars.
>
> You may not have much time to find this faded sign in the darkness before Owen Shaw finds you.

☐ Find a souvenir for the car lover inside Custom Gear

> Inside the Custom Gear shop, you will find the perfect souvenir for the car lover in your family.

Hats, clothing, sunglasses, and *Fast & the Furious* signature items can be found for fans of this thrilling film franchise.

The Wizarding World of Harry Potter™ - Diagon Alley™

As you enter the magical, mystical world of Harry Potter, you will explore the well-known shops and attractions that bring you right to the heart of the Harry Potter books. Become a wizard yourself when you don your robes, hold your wand in hand, and transport yourself to a world where anything is possible.

Make a deposit at Gringotts™ or grab a bite at the Leaky Cauldron before racing through the vaults below the famous Gringotts™ bank.

Be very careful, or you may take a wrong turn and wind up in the dark and mystic Knockturn Alley™.

☐ Travel through King's Cross Station

> As you walk through Universal Studios Florida, you will come to King's Cross Station. Check the departures and arrivals before working your way

through the impressive station on your way to the Platform 9 ¾.

As you work your way through the brick station, you will see luggage waiting to be loaded on the next train leaving London or even heading towards the famous Hogwarts™ castle.

☐ Pose for pictures with the Divine Magic billboard

Guests walking through King's Cross Station will come to the massive Divine Magic advertisement. Fans of the Harry Potter series of films may recognize this billboard from *Harry Potter and the Half-Blood Prince* when Harry finds Dumbledore in the subway station.

☐ Get video of you walking through the wall to Platform 9 ¾

You will come to a large luggage cart as you walk through the train station on the second floor. If you watch as other guests come to the opposite side of this cart, they magically walk through the wall to the hidden platform beyond.

Be sure to get someone to take a video of you performing this bit of magic yourself.

☐ Walk through the wall to Platform 9 ¾

> Everyone who has read a Harry Potter book or seen the films has dreamed of walking through the wall to Platform 9 ¾ and now it is your turn.
>
> You will hear the brick give way as you navigate the wall trusting that you will make it to the other side and arrive on the Platform for the Hogwarts Express™.

☐ Get a picture with Hedwig, the owl

> As you arrive on Platform 9 ¾, you will walk around a group of luggage on the platform waiting to be loaded on the Hogwarts Express™. Among the luggage, you will find Harry's owl Hedwig waiting for his owner. Watch as Hedwig turns his head from side to side and get a picture with this famous owl before traveling on the train.

☐ Ride the Hogwarts Express™

> When the Hogwarts Express™ arrives in the station and you are seated in your private compartment, you will be whisked away to the magical world of Harry Potter™. See your favorite characters as you travel from London across the countryside to a world where wizards and magical creatures live.

Keep an eye out for your favorite characters on the train, but beware of the Dementors. Once your train arrives at Hogsmeade™, you will find Hagrid waiting for you on the Platform.

☐ Dial MAGIC in the phone booth

On the street outside King's Cross Station, you will find a red phone booth standing quietly on the street. Step inside and lift the receiver. Dial the numbers that spell out MAGIC and listen to the recording.

The voice will inform you that you have reached the Ministry of Magic. This is just another bit of magic in the muggle world.

☐ Find the album cover for *Here's to Swimming with Bow Legged Women*

On the street near King's Cross Station, you will find a record store on the street. Displayed in the window are many albums for sale. Among them is an album cover with the song *Swimmin' with Bow Legged Women* by the Quint Trio.

This album is a tribute to the attraction previously housed in this area, Jaws. For fans of the film *Jaws*, Quint Brody and Hooper are on the Orca singing this song while hunting the killer shark, and now Universal set designers have included this cover as a reminder of the beloved attraction.

☐ Take a picture with the Knight Bus

Near the water stands a large blue double-decker bus. Fans of the Harry Potter films will recognize this as the Knight Bus that Harry climbs aboard in *Harry Potter and the Prisoner of Azkaban*.

Now you can get your picture taken with this famous bus too.

☐ Talk with Dre Head

As you walk to the Knight Bus and see the bus driver, his diminutive copilot is waiting to have a conversation with you. Dre Head is a great conversationalist and loves to tell jokes to guests posing for pictures with him.

Next time you see Dre Head, ask for a high five, and watch his reaction.

☐ Admire the Alfred Gilbert Eros Fountain

Near the Knight Bus™, guests will find the elaborate Eros Fountain designed by Alfred Gilbert. This fountain is a smaller replica of the original found in Piccadilly Circus in London.

Be sure to get some fantastic souvenir photos with this beautiful fountain.

☐ Find Kreacher the house-elf watching you

Across from the Knight Bus, you will find a row of neighborhood homes. Look at the windows on the second floor, and you may find Kreacher the house-elf peering out at you from behind the curtains only to pull them closed again, so he is not seen by muggles.

☐ Walk through the wall to Diagon Alley™

Guests walking through the area around the Knight Bus may not even realize there is a whole other magical world just beyond the wall.

Find the building across from the Knight Bus and walk through the opening to find the wall to Diagon Alley™ open and ready for you to come through.

Listen as you walk through the wall, and you can hear the bricks moving.

☐ See the sign at the Leaky Cauldron

The famous Leaky Cauldron invites you with the cracked cauldron sign, look closer this sign is a leaky cauldron that drip water on unsuspecting guests walking beneath.

☐ Eat at the Leaky Cauldron

> Fan of the Harry Potter film have seen their favorite characters from these films eating at the Leaky Cauldron in London, and now you can join them to try the cuisine.
>
> Step through the door and order your favorite fish and chips, Beef Lamb and Guinness stew or Bangers and Mash to satisfy your hunger.
>
> Take your enchanted candlestick to your table, and your food will magically appear.

☐ Read the closing instructions at the Leaky Cauldron

> Near the exit, you will find a notice attached to the wall. Take some time to read this tongue in cheek notice to find out how to leave after the witching hour.

☐ Shop at Quality Quidditch™ Supplies

> Step inside Quality Quidditch™ Supplies and pick out your gear for your next match on the Quidditch™ field. Everything from sweaters, scarves, T-shirts, and caps can be found within this small shop in Diagon Alley™ so stop by on your next visit.

Weasley's Wizard Wheezes

☐ Find the magic rabbit at Weasley's Wizard Wheezes

> As you stand before the bright orange shop for Weasley's Wizard Wheezes, you will see one of the Weasley brothers larger than life on the building. As he tips his hat, you will be surprised to see a rabbit magically appear and disappear with each tip of his top hat.

☐ Watch the enchantment on the ceiling of Weasley's Wizard Wheezes

> Step into Weasley's Wizard Wheezes and look straight up to the ceiling. The Weasley brothers have been busy using their magic to enchant the ceiling with a constant barrage of fireworks going off to create a dazzling display inside this shop.

☐ Explore Weasley's Wizard Wheezes for your next toy or gag

> The walls of Weasley's are stacked with the latest toys and gags stocked by the Weasley twins. Whether you are looking for puking pastilles, extendable ears, or Pygmy Puffs, you will find your heart's desire at Weasley's Wizard Wheezes.

☐ Find Delores Umbridge inside Weasley's Wizard Wheezes

> Delores Umbridge, placed by the Ministry of Magic to watch over Hogwarts™ school, was hated by the student body, so the Weasley brothers have created a toy to poke fun at this powerful woman.
>
> Now, the Weasley's have immortalized her in toy form, and you can find her high above your head balancing on the high wire balancing two cauldrons.
>
> Guests can take her home to continue her torment in their homes.

Gladrags Wizardwear™

☐ Check out the mirror in Gladrags Wizardwear™

> Within Gladrags Wizardwear™, you will find a mirror, unlike any other. Walk through this shop and stand before the full-length mirror in the center of the shop, and you will get more than a reflection.
>
> This mirror will speak to you, letting you know how beautiful you are or what you need to change

depending on its mood, so be careful before walking up to this truthful mirror.

☐ Find the enchanted gown in Gladrags Wizardwear™

Gladrags Wizardwear™ offers clothing for every wizard, including the stunning white gown displayed on the mannequin in the center of the room.

Walk around this beautiful gown, and you will find out the gown is enchanted with delicate flowers flowing down the train and fading into the fabric right before your eyes. The wizards at Gladrags know just how to make the perfect gown to fit your imagination.

☐ Look in the window of the Jellied Eel & Mashed Onion Shop

Throughout Diagon Alley, muggles will find the strange or unusual. Look in the window of the Jellied Eel & Mashed Onion shop, and you will see eels in various forms, including a literal eel pie with their little heads poking out.

☐ Find the Monster Book of Monsters in the window of the book store

Just around the corner from the Jellied Eel is the book store with the famous Monster Book of Monsters™ tearing the other poor books to pieces.

Stop and watch this terrifying scene of book carnage that has finally been caught and now creates destruction within the window of the book shop.

☐ Visit Globus Mundi travel agency

The Globus Mundi travel agency is opened and waiting for you to come in and find your new vacation getaway.

While inside this shop, you can find everything from keychains to pins dedicated to the world of Harry Potter.

☐ Visit Shutterbugs for more than a picture

Fans of the Harry Potter films know when someone has their picture taken, the picture captures their movements apart from the photo itself. Now you can get one of your very own when you step into Shutterbugs to pose for your pictures.

☐ Knock on the door of the Daily Prophet™

The famous Daily Prophet™ reporters are working hard behind the door in Diagon Alley™. Raise the brass door knocker and then listen carefully as you can hear the staff working away.

☐ Watch the self-knitting needles at Spindlewarps

> Enchanted objects are for sale in every shop in Diagon Alley™. Stop at Spindlewarps and watch the self-knitting needles demonstrate their talents. The pattern on the needles should be recognizable to fans of the Harry Potter series of films as the pattern Mrs. Weasley was creating with her own set of self-knitting needles.

☐ Find the shark jaw in the window of Slug & Jiggers Apothecary

> Slug & Jiggers offers a wide array of items to be used in spells, hexes, and charms. Hidden among the various jars stands alone sharks jaw that is not noticed by most guests.
>
> This sharks jaw is more than set decoration, and this is another souvenir from the Jaws attraction that was seen in this area of Universal Studios Florida, before the Harry Potter universe took up residence.

☐ Read the various signage throughout Diagon Alley™

> While there are many shops that guests in Diagon Alley™ can step into and explore, the signage throughout this magical street hints at so many more that are not available to the public. Read

the signs throughout Diagon Alley™ to find your favorites from the Harry Potter universe.

Ollivanders™

☐ Find the enchanted broom at Ollivanders™

> Step in the door of Ollivanders™ wand shop and the first thing you may notice is the enchanted broom running amok while sweeping the ceiling. This broom has been sweeping for so long that there is nothing but bare wood above the ever-sweeping bristles.

☐ Attend a wand fitting at Ollivanders™

> Every new wizard dreams of getting their wand fitting at Ollivanders™, and now you have your chance to be selected by the wand fitter during the Ollivanders™ wand fitting demonstration.
>
> The wand master will select a young student and find the perfect wand to fit the new wizard.

☐ Find the core items for wands in the window of Ollivanders™

> Look in the window of Ollivanders, and you will find the items that bring wands to life. In the glass jars, you will find unicorn hairs, dragon

heartstrings, and phoenix feathers waiting to be used in the next wand.

Harry Potter and the Escape from Gringotts™

☐ Take a picture of the stack of gold statue outside Gringotts™ Bank

> Outside Gringotts™, you will find a giant statue of a stack of gold with a goblin standing atop this glittering money. Get a fun picture with this statue as a memory of your trip to Gringotts™ Bank.

☐ Watch the dragon on top of Gringotts™ Bank blow fire

> The jewel in the crown of Diagon Alley™ is Gringotts™ Bank, but it has been taken over by an enormous fire breathing dragon. Listen, and you will hear this gargantuan dragon growl before blowing a huge plume of fire above Diagon Alley™.
>
> Unfortunately, there are times this dragon is not feeling like showing off, so there are times you make not get her to cooperate.

- [ ] Walk through Gringotts™ bank

    Enter Gringotts™ Bank and walk through the stunning bank where the goblins are busy at work counting money and processing deposits. Look up and see a stunning crystal chandelier as you work your way to the vaults and offices.

    As you pass the goblin towards the end of the room, he will speak to give instructions to those wishing to access the vaults.

- [ ] Survive a trip through the vaults on Harry Potter and the Escape from Gringotts™

    Climb aboard a train to visit the vaults beneath Gringotts™ Bank, but this trip is anything but ordinary. Watch yourself as you encounter the vault security guards, a fire breathing dragon, and Lord Voldemort before your ride is through.

    Pray you make it back alive.

- [ ] See your Gringotts™ photograph

    Be sure to stop and see the photo of you taken by the Gringotts™ staff as you walked through the hallways of Gringotts™. You will have an opportunity to purchase this memory of your day at Gringotts™ Banks if you choose to.

- [ ] Try an ice cream at Florean Fortescue's Ice-cream Parlour

    Across from the Harry Potter and the Escape from Gringotts™ attraction, you will find Florean Fortescue's Ice-cream Parlour. Select from soft serve or traditional ice cream in a waffle cone or souvenir glass.

    Whether your taste buds crave Chocolate Chili, Salted Caramel Blondie, or Earl Grey and Lavender, you will find something cold at Florean Fortescue's Ice Cream Parlour to satisfy your sweet tooth.

- [ ] Visit Magical Menagerie for a new wizarding pet

    For guests looking for a new pet to take home from Diagon Alley™, step into Magical Menagerie and find the perfect companion.

    Everything from Pygmy Puffs to Cornish Pixies can be found within this small shop.

    Also available for adoption are some of your favorite pets from the Harry Potter wizards. Crookshanks™, Scabbers™, and Hedwig™ can be found on the shelves waiting for their forever home.

☐ Find the serpent speaking Parseltongue

> In the side window of Magical Menagerie is housed a gigantic serpent waiting for someone to adopt him. If you listen carefully, you will hear this serpent speak Parseltongue, the language only heard by wizards who speak Parseltongue.

☐ Grab a Butterbeer™ at The Fountain of Fair Fortune™

> Step inside The Fountain of Fair Fortune™ where you can get an ice-cold Butterbeer™ in a collector mug, or perhaps you prefer a pumpkin juice or Gillywater to give you energy for your day.
>
> Guests will find a wide variety of thirst-quenching items named after your favorite characters from the Tales of Beedle the Bard within this bar, so step up and order your favorite.
>
> For those looking for something stronger, try a Fishy Green Ale.

☐ Bring the rain with a magic spell

> As you explore Diagon Alley™, you will come across a black umbrella suspended in the air. Cast a spell with your interactive wand, and the umbrella will begin to make it rain on Diagon Alley™.

☐ Find the Skelegrow display

> Towards a back corner of Diagon Alley™, you will find a window with a display of Skelegrow Elixir. Fans of the Harry Potter films remember when the Hogwarts™ nurse gave this Elixir to Harry to grow the bone in his arm back after an unfortunate interaction with Gilderoy Lockhart.
>
> Unfortunately, you cannot purchase this Elixir for yourself, but the advertisement is a wonderful reminder of this enchanted potion used in the world of Harry Potter.

Knockturn Alley™

☐ Walk through the dark streets of Knockturn Alley

> Hidden from the rest of Diagon Alley™ is the entrance to the dark and sinister Knockturn Alley™.
>
> Step into the darkness where evil lurks in every corner. Here you will discover your nightmares have become a reality, so tread carefully as you explore Knockturn Alley™.

One Hundred Things to do at Walt Disney World Before you Die

☐ Use your interactive wand to make Knockturn Alley™ come to life

> Your interactive wand provides you the ability to be a wizard, and Knockturn Alley™ is no different. Point your wand towards the lock to magically turn the dials, but be warned, this lock may defend itself. Interact with the shrunken heads and listen to them sing or tell jokes.
>
> You never know what may come to life when you cast these dark arts spells within Knockturn Alley™.

Borgin and Burkes™

☐ Visit Borgin and Burkes™

> Step in the door of Borgin and Burkes™ to find everything a wizard turning to the dark could need.
>
> Whether you are looking for clothing, decorations, or accessories to complete your dark arts training, stop in a Borgin and Burkes™ on your next visit to Knockturn Alley™.

☐ Find the vanishing cabinet

> As you explore Borgin and Burkes™, head to the back corner to the right side of the cash register area, and you will find a large cabinet, but this item is not for sale.
>
> Fans of the Harry Potter films remember Draco Malfoy™ using this cabinet to travel from Hogwarts™ to Knockturn Alley™ to bring Death Eaters™ into the castle.
>
> Press your ear to the cabinet, and you can hear the bird still within.

☐ Find the trunk with the Boggart trapped inside

> Beneath one of the counters within Borgin and Burkes™, you will find a trunk that rattles and moves.
>
> Listen carefully, and you will hear the Boggart within the trunk, trying desperately to free itself. These shapeshifters are a wizard's worst nightmare, so its best to leave this one right where he is.

☐ Find the troll foot umbrella stand

> If you look at the items stored atop the cabinets in Borgin and Burkes™, you will find an extremely large umbrella stand. Look carefully, and you will

see that this is no ordinary piece of furniture; it is a repurposed troll foot.

☐ Find the broken china doll

Inside the cabinets, you will find many disturbing items used for the dark arts. On one of the upper shelves, you will find a china doll that has seen better days. This poor doll has many cracks and two areas that are broken with pieces missing.

If you look very closely in the fading light, you will notice this doll is much more than she appears to be. Observe the broken areas, and you will find a skeleton beneath the porcelain.

☐ Find the cursed hand in the cabinets of Borgin and Burkes™

Encased within a glass case on a shelf in a quiet corner of Borgin and Burkes™ stands an object more dangerous than anything else.

Read the sign in front of the cursed hand for a solemn warning for all who are tempted to touch this cursed item.

- [ ] Listen to the shrunken heads perform at Noggin and Bonce

    Near Borgin and Burkes™, you will find a window with a unique display. Walk closer to find several shrunken heads hanging in the window of Noggin and Bonce.

    Wave your interactive wand and watch these heads come back to life and sing for you, as well as tell jokes.

- [ ] Find the mermaid skeleton at Dystyl Phaelanges

    In the window of Dystyl Phaelanges, you will find the bones of many creatures, but the most unusual has a position of honor. Find the full mermaid skeleton hanging high up in the window showing these mythical creatures do exist in the world of Harry Potter™.

- [ ] Watch the enchanted skeleton at Dystyl Phaelanges

    Watch as the skeleton diagram displayed within Dystyl Phaelanges comes to life with a wave of your wand.

    Once you cast your spell, the gorilla will move along with you as you wave your arms or dance around. You are in charge when you step up to the window of Dystyl Phaelanges.

☐ Explore the decorative bone displays

> The talented artists at Dystyl Phaelanges have taken the art of display to a whole new level. Check out the ceiling of this shop to see the elaborate configuration of long bones and rib cages suspended from the ceiling.
>
> Even the sign of this shop has many bones attached. There is no question as to the specialty of this shop.

☐ Find the house-elf in the chimney sweep sign

> The house-elves are used by the best wizarding families to make life easier, and the chimney sweep sign is no different.
>
> This usual sign shows the inner workings of a chimney, but the actual advertising comes when you point your wand to the sign and watch the little house-elf climb up and down within the chimney.

☐ Read the business signs throughout Knockturn Alley™

> Throughout Knockturn Alley™, you will find signs for unusual business that would not be found anywhere else in Diagon Alley™.

E.L.M. Undertakers & Embalmers, Flederman's and Tanner Bats and Skins and the Nocturnal Venomous Arachnid shop are just a few of the oddities you will find throughout this dark area.

☐ Find the Phoenix Fire Lighters advertisement

Very high on the wall closest to the Leaky Cauldron™ as you exit Knockturn Alley™, you will find an advertisement for Phoenix Fire Lighters. Keep an eye out as this advertisement will disappear right before your eyes.

☐ Read the advertisements on the walls of Weasley's Wizarding Wheezes

As you work your way back to Weasley's Wizarding Wheezes, you will notice many advertisements painted on the brick on the side and back of this shop. These advertisements show the various products that can be found within Weasley's.

☐ Visit Sugar Plum's Sweet Shop

For guests looking for something sweet, stop at Sugar Plum's Sweet Shop for a wide variety of sweets for every taste in the wizarding world.

Try the pink coconut ice or exploding bonbons. The fresh-made cauldron cakes are a favorite along with the fizzing whizbees.

For guests looking for something unusual, try the acid pops or a Shock-O-Choc.

☐ Find the statue of Dobby the house-elf

High above the doorways near Sugar Plum's Sweet Shop, you will find a tiny statue of Dobby, the brave little house elf. Dobby worked his way into the hearts of every Harry Potter fan, and now he is immortalized in Diagon Alley™.

☐ Find the owls house above the Owl Post™

The Owl Post™ delivers thousands of pieces of mail by owl, and now you can see how the owls live just above the Owl Post™ sign. These enclosed spaces offer protection from the elements when the owls are not making deliveries all over the world.

You can also see how long the owls have been in residence by the number of droppings on the building.

- [ ] Visit Wands by Gregorovitch

    The rival to Ollivander™ is Gregorovich in Diagon Alley™. Here you can find a wide array of wands made by this talented wandmaker who crafted the wand used by none other than Victor Krum.

    Stop by this shop to see if Gregorovitch has your perfect wand.

- [ ] Step up to the mermaid fountain

    Stand before the mermaid fountain and use your interactive wand to cast your Aquamenti™ spell. If you cast your spell correctly, the fountain will come to life and squirt the one casting the spell and anyone unlucky enough to be standing in the wrong spot.

- [ ] Visit Brown E. Wrights Blacksmith shop

    Near the Owl Post™, you will find Brown E. Wrights Blacksmith shop where the Golden Snitch™ was created. Stand before the open door, and you can use your interactive wand to move the bellows or repair the suit of armor within the shop.

☐ Try a cold beverage at the Hopping Pot

> In a quiet corner of Diagon Alley™, guests can walk up to the counter of the Hopping Pot and get a cold Butterbeer™, for a special treat try a frozen Butterbeer™ or Butterbeer™ ice cream. The Hopping Pot offers guests a variety of non-alcoholic drinks to satisfy any taste.
>
> For guests looking for something alcoholic, try a Dragon Scales Beer or Fishy Green Ale.

☐ Watch the performance of The Tales of Beedle the Bard

> Stand before the stage in Diagon Alley™ and watch as the talented students of the Wizarding Academy of Dramatic Arts™ perform two of the stories from The Tales of Beedle the Bard for you. Working with intricate puppets and scenery, they will make these tales come to life to entertain you.
>
> Be sure to be in the audience for this amazing show on your next trip to Diagon Alley™.

☐ See Celestina Warbeck and the Banshees

> Celestina Warbeck has brought her show to Diagon Alley™, and now she and her backup singers, the Banshees, are ready to perform for you.

Listen as they perform your favorite wizarding songs in this outdoor stage in Diagon Alley™.

- [ ] Explore the Museum of Muggle Curiosities

    The wizarding world has a unique museum in Diagon Alley™. Be sure to peek in the window of the Museum of Muggle Curiosities to see how the muggle world managed to function without magic.

    Radios, microwaves, vacuum cleaners, and telephones can be found within the window for the wizards to marvel at while they try to imagine the world where there is no magic.

- [ ] Visit Gringotts™ Money Exchange

    Step in the door of Gringotts™ Money Exchange, where you can get a truly unique souvenir of your time in the wizarding world. Step up to the counter and exchange your muggle money for wizarding currency at a one to one exchange rate.

    While in this annex of Gringotts™ Bank, you can have a conversation with the goblin, and he will answer your questions. Be sure to ask good questions, or he will dismiss you.

You can get other great Gringotts™ merchandise souvenirs that are not found in other shops, so be sure to stop by on your next trip to Diagon Alley™.

☐ Stop at Eternelle's Elixir of Refreshment

This large kiosk in Diagon Alley™ offers guests a beverage that goes beyond refreshment. Step up and select your desired potion from Fire Protection, Babbling Beverage, Draught of Peace, or Elixir to Induce Euphoria.

The potion master will mix your Elixir into your Gillywater, and you will feel the potion working with the first sip.

☐ Find your wizarding stationery within Scribbulus

Letter writing takes on a whole new dimension when you get your stationery supplies at Scribbulus.

Whether you are looking for quills, house stationery, sealing wax and stamps, or journals, Scribbulus has everything you need.

The shelves are stocked with a complete product line for each house, so you will be representing your house in style.

- [ ] Find your magical supplies at Wiseacre's Wizarding Equipment

    For new wizards, step into Wiseacre's Wizarding Equipment and find everything you need for the school year.

    Wiseacre's offers a supply of clothing along with time turners, crystal balls, hourglasses, and much more.

World Expo

Go back in time to the 1964 Worlds Fair as you enter a world where you can face your biggest fears on stage for the world to see.

Join the Men in Black™ as they save the Earth from alien attacks. Join them for your on-the-job training and see if you can join their ranks.

If you can complete your training by outshooting your fellow trainees, you will earn your status as one of the top Men in Black.

☐ Volunteer for Fear Factor Live

> Guests can volunteer to face their darkest fears by joining the cast of Fear Factor Live. Get to the stage early to volunteer and be led through a series of challenges to test your physical and mental strength.
>
> Do you have what it takes to be the last one standing? Join the cast to find out.

☐ Find the last remnants of the 1964 World's Fair

> The observatory towers are the last standing structures from the 1964 World's Fair. Little did the earth know that these structures hold a secret.
>
> These are interstellar spacecraft hidden in plain sight, so get your pictures before they fly away.

Men in Black™: Alien Attack

☐ Walk through the Men in Black™ headquarters

> Enter the headquarters of the Men in Black™ and enter a world where anything can happen. As you explore the hallways of this top-secret training facility, read the signage for the different departments.
>
> As you work your way to the break room, do not be surprised if you find some aliens operating the coffee machine. Be sure to stop at the bulletin board to read the notices and comics the personnel has posted.
>
> Finally, enter the weapon room where the Men in Black™ select their weapons to protect the Earth.

☐ Save the planet from aliens on Men in Black™ Alien Attack

> Step aboard your vehicle and start your training to become the newest member of the Men in Black™. As you work your way through the training grounds, aim your weapon to take out the aliens and raise your score.
>
> Keep your wits about you as you never know what can happen during your training.

☐ Get your Men in Black™ gear at MIB gear

> As you exit the Men in Black™ facility, stop at the gift shop to find your new gear. Whether you are looking for clothing, toys, or collectibles, you will find your new favorite souvenir at MIB Gear.

☐ Take a tour of the immigration room at Men in Black™ Alien Attack

> Guests have the chance to visit the first floor of the immigration room of Men in Black™. Explore the first floor where you can sit at the desks, pose for pictures with the immigration aliens or sit in the lounge area.
>
> This tour is not always available and subject to staff availability, so ask at the entrance of the attraction for the tour.

☐ Stop at the Coke™ Freestyle refill station

> Near the Men in Black™ Alien Attack, you will find one of the Coke™ Freestyle refill stations where you can top off your souvenir cups. This station is unique as you can step into the air-conditioned comfort and rest on comfortable couches for a few minutes to rest from your busy day.

Springfield: Home of the Simpsons

Hang out with your friends the Simpson's when you step into Springfield. Explore the games of Krustyland or stop in the Kwik-E-Mart for an ice-cold Squishee. Get a picture with Bart, Lisa, Homer, and Marge or dare to meet Sideshow Bob.

Wind up your day with an ice-cold drink at Moe's Tavern as you immerse yourself in the world of the Simpson's.

☐ Try your hand at the Simpsons™ Games

> Step right up and try your hand at games of skill at the Simpsons™ Games. Try a dog race, shoot some hoops, throw the baseballs, or whack the rats to win fun Simpsons™ themed prizes you cannot get anywhere else.

The Simpsons Ride™

☐ Find Krusty's uvula

As you walk through the mouth of Krusty the Clown to enter the queue for the Simpson's Ride™, look up at the roof of Krusty's mouth. You will find Krusty's uvula, the little piece of flesh that hangs above the throat.

☐ Read the advertisements for the attractions at Krustyland

As you work your way through the queue for the Simpson's Ride™, read some of the advertisements for the attractions and shows at Krustyland.

You will recognize some of your favorite Simpson's characters in the shows and rides you will experience at Krustyland.

☐ Watch the clips from the Simpsons while in the queue for the Simpson's Ride

Watch the monitors to see clips from your favorite episodes of the Simpsons. The Simpson's know how to grow your excitement for Krustyland by showing your favorite moments from the past, so enjoy this look back at the Simpsons.

☐ Check out the booths in the pre-show for The Simpson's Ride

> As you arrive at the preshow area, look around at the booths surrounding you.
>
> Hans Moleman works the information booth while Patty and Selma work the lost and found. Try some of the theme park food or try the games with Groundkeeper Willie.

☐ Survive a day at Krustyland and stop Sideshow Bob

> Step in the ride vehicle and start on this wild ride while you try to survive an attack from Sideshow Bob.
>
> Ride the rollercoaster, join the happy little elves, and see the water show as you run for your life. It is anyone's guess which one of the Simpson's will save you from Sideshow Bob.

☐ Ride Kang and Kodos' Twirl 'N' Hurl

> Those aliens Kang and Kodos' have been tormenting the Simpsons every Halloween for years, and now it is your turn on Kang and Kodos' Twirl 'N' Hurl. Hop in an alien spacecraft and go round and round while trying to hold onto your lunch.

Be sure to read the names of the space ships for a giggle.

Duff Brewery

☐ Stop at Duff Brewery for a cold drink

> Duff Brewery is open and waiting for you to step up to the bar for an ice-cold Duff. This open-air bar offers a great view of the lake while you rest as you sip your Duff or Duff Lite, or a frozen Strawberry Margarita.
>
> Top off your time at Duff Brewery with a sandwich or snack.

☐ Get a picture with Duffman

> Duffman, the iconic spokesman for Duff Brewery, is standing outside, waiting to be in your pictures. This Duffman statue stands in his blue tights with his dug beer can belt and red cape.
>
> Meet this honest to goodness celebrity at Duff Brewery.

☐ Get pictures with the seven Duffs

> Standing outside the Duff Brewery, you will find the seven Duffs. Fans of the Simpsons may remember the characters from Duff Gardens, and now they have come to Springfield to pose for pictures with you.
>
> Pick your favorite from Edgy, Dizzy, Tipsy, Surly, Queasy, Sleazy, or Remorseful.

The Kwik-E-Mart

☐ Pick up the payphone in front of the Kwik-E-Mart

> On the side of the Kwik-E-Mart stand a payphone that will not connect you to any phone number outside of Springfield.
>
> Pick up the receiver and listen to the voice on the other end of the phone, make prank phone calls to the Kwik-E-Mart.
>
> Listen closely, and you may recognize the voice as Nelson, one of Bart and Lisa's classmates.

☐ Get a picture with Milhouse in front of the Kwik E Mart

> Sitting on the bench outside the Kwik-E-Mart enjoying an ice-cold Squishee sits Milhouse, Bart's best friend. Pose for a picture with this adorable character before it is time for him to go home.

☐ Read the advertisements in the window of the Kwik-E-Mart

> The Kwik-E-Mart offers products everyone in Springfield needs, so just look through the window to find just what you need.
>
> Whether it is cat litter, Krusty O's, Chutney Squishees, or diapers, you will find the products everyone is using.
>
> Spend some time reading the packages or signs to get a chuckle before heading in to do your shopping.

☐ Pop into the Kwik-E-Mart for a snack or a souvenir

> Stop in the Kwik-E-Mart to find the perfect gift for that special someone from Springfield. Inside you will find great Simpson's T-shirts, Duff items, toys, or the iconic giant pink donut.

Toys for the little ones or pins, including the elusive Bort license plate from Krustyland.

☐ Stop at the Fast Food Avenue for a bite to eat

When you are ready for something to eat during your time in Springfield, stop at Fast Food Avenue to find the perfect item.

Inside, you will find Luigi's Pizza, Cletus Chicken Shack, the Frying Dutchman, or Lisa's Teahouse of Horror for your favorites. Be sure to find Lisa's signature saxophone mounted on the wall of her teahouse.

Sit in air-conditioned comfort while you watch your favorite clips from Simpson's episodes.

☐ Find all of the Simpsons characters in the mural at Fast Food Avenue

Inside Fast Food Avenue, you will find a mural spanning the length of one wall showing life in Springfield. Examine the mural to find all of your favorite Springfielders living their life.

You may find some sidesplitting moments caught along the way.

Moe's Tavern

☐ Sit at the bar at Moe's Tavern

> Moe's Tavern is open and waiting for you to sit at the bar to get a cold drink. Ask the bartender to pour you a cold Duff or a Flaming Moe. Pose for a picture with Barney as he stares into his empty glass or sits at the pool table.
>
> Be sure to look around at the memorabilia around the room or read the bottles behind the bar for some amusement.

☐ Pick up the phone on the bar at Moe's Tavern

> At the end of the bar, you will find a bright red phone. Pick up the receiver and listen to Bart Simpson prank call Moe.
>
> Keep picking up the phone and listen to a different joke each time you answer.

☐ Get a picture with Barney from The Simpson's

> Barney is standing, waiting for his glass to refill inside Moe's Tavern. While he is distracted, get a picture with this larger than life character during your time inside Moe's Tavern.

- [ ] Get a picture of Jebediah Springfield, founder of Springfield

    Standing near Duff Brewery stands the statue of Springfield founder Jebediah Springfield. Standing with the bear he claims to have beaten; the statue was erected to honor this embiggened man.

- [ ] Get a picture with Chief Wiggum and his dented police car

    Standing outside Lard Lad Donuts is Chief Wiggum, having a donut and cup of coffee. Clearly, he was in a hurry since he crashed his police car into a fire hydrant, and the hydrant is spraying water all over the area.

    Get a picture with the Chief before he finishes his donut.

- [ ] Get a giant donut at Lard Lad Donuts

    There is only one donut shop in Springfield, Lard Lad Donuts. The giant Lard Lad stands high above Springfield, beckoning guests to come in and buy the giant donuts, including the class pink donut, the favorite of Homer Simpson.

    If you are looking for something cold, try the ice cream at Lard Lad.

☐ Get a snack at the Bumblebee Man Taco Truck

> Bumblebee Man has his food truck parked in Springfield, waiting for guests to try his signature Mexican food. Try a nacho plate or tacos in many flavors.
>
> Be sure to get your food before Bumblebee Man is needed on the set at channel Ocho.

Central Park

☐ Take a walk around Central Park

> Guests looking for a quiet place to relax during their time at Universal Studios Florida will find the perfect opportunity in Central Park. The large tree-covered area offers a spectacular view of the theme park with plenty of benches to rest.
>
> During the Cinematic Celebration show, the Central Park area will be crowded with guests, so get your seat early.

☐ Find the DeLorean from *Back to the Future*

> Near the Central Park area, you can come face to face with one of the most recognizable picture cars in cinematic history. The DeLorean from *Back to the Future* is parked near the walkway by Central Park, and you can pose for pictures with this time travel vehicle.

☐ Find the Jules Verne train from *Back to the Future III*

> Fans of the *Back to the Future* films remember the climactic final scene when Doc Brown arrives in the train engine you see before you near Central Park. This screen used engine is now on permanent display for guests to pose for pictures.

Woody Woodpecker's KidZone

Go back to the age of classic cartoons as you explore the Woody Woodpecker KidZone. Visit Woody Woodpecker and his niece and nephew as you race along. Spend some time with everyone's favorite purple dinosaur Barney or get soaked with Curious George as you step into the pages of a storybook.

Play with Fievel and his friends as you shrink down to the size of a mouse and top off your time with a ride on a flying bike at the E.T. Adventure.

☐ See a performance of Animal Actors on Location!

> See these talented animal performers show off their skills that brought them fame on the big screen in this delightful show.
>
> Dogs, cats, birds, and various other animal performers take the stage alongside their trainers to demonstrate how the training process begins that help these animal actors to navigate the filming process.

If you are lucky, you may be selected to assist the trainers on the stage.

☐ Explore SpongeBob StorePants

SpongeBob has taken up residence at Universal Studios Florida, and now you can shop for your SpongeBob merchandise.

Everything from T-shirts to toys can be found, so take some time to find the perfect souvenir from Bikini Bottom.

Be sure to spend some time reading the signs posed by Mr. Crabbs; he has been busy making sure the guests know the rules in his store.

☐ Pose for pictures with SpongeBob and his friends

Within SpongeBob StorePants, guests will find the famous sponge ready to pose for pictures along with his friend Patrick. Get your cameras ready to get pictures with these famous friends from beneath the sea.

☐ Enjoy a slice of pizza at the KidZone Pizza Company

For guests looking for their favorite flavor of pizza, stop at the KidZone Pizza Company in the Woody Woodpecker KidZone.

Take some time to sit in comfort while you enjoy your meal. The KidZone Pizza Company has something for everyone in the family.

The E.T. Adventure

- [ ] Ride on a bike to save E.T.

    Travel on a flying bike to help E.T. save his home planet. Travel through the forest, but be sure to keep one step ahead of the government agents trying to take E.T. from you. Arrive on his home planet and let E.T. use his healing touch to bring his friends back to health.

    Before your ride is through, you will come face to face with E.T. when he personally thanks you and everyone on your ride for helping him.

- [ ] Get a picture with E.T. in Gertie's closet or on the flying bicycle

    As you exit your E.T. adventure, you will have the opportunity to get your picture taken with E.T. inside Gerties' closet and hop aboard the flying bicycle. This special personalized souvenir can put your family right in the action of this favorite family film.

Fievel's Playland

☐ Play in Fievel's Playland

> Shrink down to the size of a mouse to join in the fun in Fievel's Playland. Climb on the oversized items, slide down the harmonica box, play on the jungle gym of playing cards along with plenty of other ways for the kids to play.
>
> Along the way, you will find a water slide, but be careful, or you will end up very wet.

A Day in the Park with Barney

☐ Play along with Barney in A Day in the Park with Barney™

> Join your favorite purple dinosaur Barney and all of his friends as they sing and dance to your favorite songs in this theater in the round.
>
> Stomp your feet and clap your hands as you sing with Barney, Baby Bop and B.J. as you play in the park.

- [ ] Play in Barney's backyard

    As you exit the show, stop to play in Barney's backyard. Step along the cobblestones to hear the noises they make. Play in the train or play among the trees.

    There is something for the little ones throughout Barney's Backyard

- [ ] Ride Woody Woodpecker's Nuthouse Coaster

    Ride with Woody Woodpecker and his niece and nephew, Splinter and Knothead, as you ride this coaster designed just for the kids.

    Read the signs left behind by this zany trio as you work your way to the loading zone. Hang on to your hat as you board your coaster and ride up and down the hills in this fun coaster for everyone in the family.

Curious George Goes to Town

- [ ] Spend time with Curious George Goes to Town

    Step through the pages of your favorite book as you play along with Curious George in Curious George goes to town. Walk through the water park as you get soaked exploring the city buildings. Play at the post office, hotel, laundry, and bank as the water overflows along the way.

Follow in the footsteps of your favorite monkey as you play in this colorful town.

Hollywood

Step onto the street of Hollywood and experience tinsel town up close and personal. Shop and eat with the stars in this glittering mecca of movies and movie stars.

Do not be surprised if you come across some of the most recognizable Hollywood stars like Marilyn Monroe or Lucille Ball. You may even see some of your favorite animated characters come to life like the gang from Scooby-Doo and the Simpsons.

Before your day in Hollywood is through, stop at the Horror Makeup show to learn the history of the horror movie industry and see the latest Hollywood make up techniques.

☐ Walk down Hollywood Blvd along the Hollywood Walk of Fame

> As you stroll along the street of Hollywood, look down at the Walk of Fame, a tribute to the movie stars that have graced the silver screen. Along the way, these pink stars show the names of some of

your favorite movie stars as well as singers and dancers.

As you read the names, be sure to check out the bronze symbol in the center of the stars. These symbols indicate either television, film, or radio.

☐ Get a burger and a shake at Mel's Diner

Join the gang at Mel's Diner for a hamburger and a frosty milkshake as you step back into the 1950s. Parked outside, you will find several classic cars from famous films. Step up and give your order, then sit in the booths to enjoy your meal and a well-deserved break from your busy day.

Universal Horror Makeup Show

☐ Walk through the Universal Horror Makeup Museum

The Horror Makeup show is an exciting behind the scenes look at the makeup effects, but the horror makeup museum in the lobby is thrilling all on its own.

Find the original makeup kit from the master of disguise Lon Chaney, Original scripts from classic horror films, bust of every recognizable monster, as well as the creatures designed by the best effect's artists in Hollywood.

Be sure to arrive early to spend some time admiring this amazing collection before the show.

☐ Go to the Universal Horror Makeup show

Take your seat as you can't miss this show during your time at Universal Studios Florida. Top Hollywood makeup artists demonstrate the history of Universal horror films while showing how these amazing effects were created.

This show is a timeline of the evolution of the horror as well as the practical effects of the horror genre. For a lucky guest, you can be selected to assist in a special effect demonstration, so get to the show early.

☐ Find one of a kind souvenirs at Williams of Hollywood

Guests can find unique souvenirs throughout Universal Studios Florida, but Williams of Hollywood offers items beyond the unusual.

Step inside and find yourself surrounded by props from retired Universal shows and attractions along with antiques from every era. Wander through this shop, and you will find items from a bygone time to take home.

☐ Become a star at the Dark Room

> Step in front of the green screen and become a star of your favorite movies at the Dark Room. This store offers a wide array of film background for you to pose in front as you become the next film star.

☐ See the Bourne Stuntacular

> Jason Bourne has come to Universal Studios Florida, and you can watch these books come to life as Bourne protects you from the sinister figures coming to stop him.
>
> Get a front-row seat for this new show that will keep you on the edge of your seat.

☐ Stop at Schwab's Drugstore for an ice cream

> Step into Schwab's Drugstore for a Ben & Jerry's™ ice cream cone and see pictures of your favorite movie stars lining the walls.
>
> This old-fashioned drug store, as a recreation of Schwab's Drug store on Sunset Blvd in Los Angeles, was rumored to be the place where star Lana Turner was discovered, but this is just a Hollywood legend. Now you can go back in time to the 1950s as you see the old-fashioned

drug store items lining the shelves as you enjoy a refreshing ice cream.

☐ Get a hat at the Brown Derby

Another Hollywood landmark along Hollywood is the Brown Derby. This Derby shaped shop offers a great variety of hats for every guest. Stop in and find everything from baseball caps to whimsical costume hats.

Be sure to read the brass plate in front of the shop embedded in the sidewalk that commemorates the Brown Derby restaurant in Los Angeles that opened in 1926 but closed its doors in 1980.

☐ Get pictures with The Simpson's

Hollywood Blvd has its share of celebrities, and the Hollywood area of Universal Studios Florida, is no different. Throughout the day, you will find the Simpson's family posing for pictures in front of their motor home parked on the street.

Be sure to get your camera ready for the first family of Springfield.

☐ Get pictures with Lucy

Celebrities are everywhere along Hollywood Blvd, so keep an eye out for everyone's favorite redhead, Lucy. Lucy is ready to pose for pictures and sign autographs in her classic blue dress, so make sure to spend some time with her next time you are walking down Hollywood Blvd.

☐ Get a picture with Betty Boop

Straight out of the cartoons, Betty Boop is waiting for you. Her black curls and bright red dress make for great pictures. She may even sing for you if you ask her nicely.

☐ Visit the Betty Boop shop

The adorable Betty Boop has her own shop, and you can stop in to get everything from this classic character.

Clothing, collectibles, jewelry, and more can be found, so stop by to see what Betty Boop has for you.

☐ Get a picture with Shaggy, Scooby and the gang

Look for the Mystery Machine parked on Hollywood Blvd, and you will find those crime fighters Fred, Thelma, Daphne, Shaggy, and their dog Scooby-Doo.

Help them solve their latest mystery, then pose for pictures before they have to leave for their next hair-raising mystery.

☐ Get a picture with Hello Kitty™

That adorable kitty Hello Kitty™ is waiting for you outside of her signature shop on Hollywood Blvd. Get ready to pose for the cutest picture anywhere at Universal Studios Florida.

☐ Stop in the Hello Kitty™ Store

The famous Hello Kitty™ has her own store at Universal Studios Florida, and now you can get everything you can imagine to take home.

T-shirts, plush toys, handbags, and more can be found within this adorable shop, so be sure to spend some time with Hello Kitty™.

Islands of Adventure

Introduction

Universal's Islands of Adventure opened in 1999 to create a whole new world of theme park attractions adjacent to the Universal Studios Florida theme park.

The park opened in addition to new resort hotels to create an all-inclusive theme park experience. With the park opening day, the worlds of Marvel, classic cartoons, Jurassic Park, Dr. Seuss, and the Lost Continent brought attraction for the entire family to enjoy.

In 2007, Universal announced that the Wizarding World of Harry Potter would find a home at this new theme park and was opened in June 2010 to huge crowds coming to see their favorite books come to life. For the first time, guests could purchase robes, wands, and accessories that came straight out of the blockbuster films they had seen.

The years that followed brought brand new attractions like Skull Island: Reign of Kong that would take guests to the mysterious Skull Islands to come face to face with the ancient King Kong. The new Hagrid's Magical Creatures Motorbike Adventure would keep guests coming back to

Universal's Islands of Adventure for more thrills from this successful franchise.

Now, Islands of Adventure continues to push the envelope with a new high-speed roller-coaster type ride with the Jurassic World theme.

Universal's Islands of Adventure has been thrilling guests for over twenty years, and it continues to bring more innovation each year.

Port of Entry™

Your adventure begins as you step through the gates of Universal's Islands of Adventure and explore the Ports of Entry™. Whether you are looking for the latest clothing styles or savor delicious chocolates, you can find them in this charming marketplace. For those looking for Christmas at any time of the year, stop by the Christmas shop to find your new favorite Christmas decorations.

Ports of Entry™ brings just a glimpse of the excitement surrounding you as you begin your day at Universal's Islands of Adventure.

☐ Visit DeFoto's Expedition Photography

> Stop in at DeFoto's Expedition Photography for all of your photography needs. Whether you use digital or traditional cameras, DeFoto's has what you need.
>
> For those looking to bring home the professional photos from photo spots throughout the theme

parks, you can view your My Universal™ photos and purchase packages.

☐ Visit the Islands of Adventure Trading Company™

The Islands of Adventure Trading Company™ offers everything you could want in one shop. Inside, you will find clothing, plush toys, collectibles, and wands from each island within the theme park all in one place.

Spend some time investigating the merchandise to pick the perfect souvenir of your time at Universal's Islands of Adventure.

☐ Find the Hoosegow Jail

As you walk along the Port of Entry™, the community is clearly an active one. Look high and low at the shops, services, and food. If you look between the building, you will find the Hoosegow Jail.

Unfortunately, the inmates have been working hard to escape, as evidence by the sheets knotted together into a makeshift rope.

☐ Find the Fire Brigade at Port of Entry™

As you walk through the Port of Entry™, look around at the signs painted on the walls. You will come to the Fire Brigade sign, but you may be disappointed that they have moved closer to the water. This may cause problems for the Port of Entry™ should a fire break out.

- [ ] Stop at the Island Market and Export™ Candy Shop

    For guests looking for something sweet, stop in the Islands Market and Export™ Candy Shop for sweets and pastries. The shelves are lined with your favorite candies while the glass cases hold an amazing variety of luscious desserts.

    Be sure to stop in to find your favorites next time you are in the Port of Entry™.

- [ ] Get pictures with the tigers or leopards

    As you walk through the Port of Entry™, you will find wild animals waiting to pose for pictures with you. Sit on a ferocious tiger or a sleek leopard for a fun picture.

- [ ] Get your caricature done

    Along the path of Port of Entry™, you will find artists waiting for guests to sit for caricatures. These talented artists will draw you and find your perfect setting for a nominal fee.

These caricatures are a great personalized souvenir, so stop in to get your portrait next time you are in the Port of Entry™.

☐ Visit the Port of Entry™ Christmas Shoppe

Guests looking for Christmas souvenirs can find great decorations at the Port of Entry™ Christmas Shoppe.

Find the perfect ornament for your tree featuring your favorite Universal characters or décor for your home.

Whether you are looking for Harry Potter, Super Hero, or Dr. Seuss themed merchandise; you will find something new for your tree.

☐ Find the kitty cats

If you look high above your head at the balconies of Port of Entry™, you will find several kitty cats lounging around.

Two of the cats are trying to get into the birdcage while two more defy gravity on the support beams high above the walkway.

☐ Find the Winit Look wheel

> The residents of Port of Entry™ are finding exciting ways to entertain themselves and the guests traveling through Port of Entry™.
>
> Look at the terraces above Port of Entry™, and you will find Winit Look with the Wheel of Fortune and various gambling games waiting for the guest to try their luck. One trick you will need to figure out the way up there.

☐ Visit the Croissant Moon Bakery

> For guests looking for a hearty treat on their way to the adventures throughout Islands of Adventure, stop at the Croissant Moon Bakery.
>
> Grab a pastry and a coffee to give you the energy you need for a full day of fun.

☐ Visit Confisco Grill

> For high-end dining, visit the Confisco Grill at Port of Entry™. While the food is excellent, the décor is worth exploring all on its own. As you enter, you may notice décor that might be better suited for other areas of the theme park.
>
> Notice the dinosaur bones, cartoon characters, and Cat in the Hats large hat stored among the

shelves. The Confisco Grill has been busy confiscating items belonging to the other residents of Islands of Adventure and now is showing them off for you during your meal.

☐ Have a drink at Backwater Bar

Guests looking for adult beverages can sit down at the Backwater Bar for an ice-cold drink. Whether you want a beer, wine, or something a little harder, the Backwater Bar has something for everyone.

☐ Visit the Navigators Club

As you come to the end of the Port of Entry, you will find a small bronze globe with Navigators Club inscribed on it. These doors hold a long-kept secret at Universal's Islands of Adventure.

For those looking for meeting space, the Navigators Club is the perfect option. Housed on the second floor, this meeting space offers spectacular views of the entirety of the Islands of Adventure.

☐ Visit the restrooms at Port of Entry™

Close to the exit of Islands of Adventure, you will find the Port of Entry ™Waterworks Authority; this is the entrance to the restrooms for those that need one final chance to relieve themselves. Like everything at Universal's Islands of Adventure, the facilities are cleverly themed.

☐ Visit the locker area

Find the large locks mounted at Stowaway Storage, and you will find the entrance to the locker area. This sign offers daily rates, but if you read the small print, they also offer yearly rates in a clever joke.

☐ Send your mail from Islands of Adventure

Near the exit of Universal's Islands of Adventure, you will find a large rocket standing in the middle of the walkway. Guests may be interested to know; the Rocket Air Mail is a functioning mailbox, and the postal service picks up three times a week.

☐ Find the love birds in Port of Entry™

Hidden in an alcove to the left of the entrance to Universal's Islands of Adventure, you may hear the soft cooing of a dove. Look in a remote corner above your head near the Islands of Adventure Trading Company™, and you will find these two small birds.

Marvel Superhero Island®

Step into the pages of your favorite Marvel comic books as you fight crime with your favorite superheroes. Ride through the city with Spider-man, meet Dr. Doom in his secret lair and visit your favorite superheroes in Marvel Super Hero Island®.

The Incredible Hulk Coaster™

☐ Find the Restricted Military Defense Lab warning on the Incredible Hulk Coaster®

> As you enter Marvel Super Hero Island®, you will cross under the Incredible Hulk Coaster®. Be sure to look up at the enclosed launch so you can see the Restricted Military Defense Lab warning from General Thaddeus Ross.
>
> Ross is known in the Marvel™ universal as the head of the project that turned Bruce Banner into the Hulk™.

☐ Listen to the Hulk's roar as the coaster takes off

> As you stand below the Incredible Hulk Coaster®, you will hear a roar with each coaster that takes off. This is the roar of none other than the Hulk.
>
> The hollow steel tubing creates this roar at the take-off. Usually, the steel is filled with concrete to quiet the sound, the developers of this attraction purposefully kept the tubing hollow to accentuate the sound.

☐ Ride the Incredible Hulk Coaster®

> Sit back and get ready for a ride while on the Incredible Hulk Coaster®. This coaster flies high above Marvel Super Hero Island® as you go through several loops at sixty-seven miles per hour.
>
> This is one of the most exciting ride at Universal's Islands of Adventure™ and a must experience for everyone.

☐ Ride Storm Force Accelatron®

> Strom has created a ride of her own offering guests of Marvel Super Hero Island® a thrilling spinning ride.

Step aboard and let Storm take you for a spin as you go faster and faster. Keep your stomach from turning over before the ride is through.

- [ ] Visit your favorite superheroes on the streets of Marvel Super Hero Island®

    Your favorite superheroes come right off the pages of the comic books you love, and they are ready to pose for pictures and sign autographs along the streets of Marvel Super Hero Island®.

    Wolverine, Spider-man, Captain America, Storm, and Rogue can be found throughout the day and arrive on their quad motorcycles to show off their awesome moves.

    For those looking for the villainous characters, Dr. Doom and Green Goblin can be found terrorizing guests but beware, or they may come for you.

- [ ] Get a picture in the Fantastic Four® Vehicle

    Standing outside Café 4™, guests can step into the Fantastic Four® vehicle and pose for pictures with the whole family.

    Be sure to get this amazing picture opportunity next time you are visiting the Café 4™.

☐ Get a superhero size meal at Café 4™

> The Fantastic Four® have opened their own café and are ready to serve you delicious meals during your time at Marvel Super Hero Island®.
>
> Stop in to sample the delicious entrees and cold drinks while you take a rest stop from the busy day.

☐ Find the Baxter Annex sign within Café 4™

> Look around Café 4™, and you will find the sign that reads Baxter Annex. Fans of the Fantastic Four comic books remember this as the residence for these superheroes in New York City.

☐ Find the Crime Update Line on the street

> Keep a close eye out for the red and yellow phone on the street and lift the receiver to hear a list of options to report crimes you witness during your day at Marvel Super Hero Island®.

Doctor Doom's Fearfall®

☐ Find Norman Osborn Industries

> As you turn down Doom Alley, you will come to the Norman Osborn building. Fans of the Spider-

man® comic books know Norman Osborn is none other than the supervillain, Green Goblin.

☐ Press the button on the yellow Doomnet

> To the right of the entrance to Doctor Dooms' Fearfall®, you will find a bright yellow call box. Press the button to hear the superheroes checking in, and Doctor Doom is listening in to find out where they will be next. Press this button several times to hear the voices of your favorite superheroes as they check-in.

☐ Hear the villains planning their next job in the alley

> Step into the alcove beneath the Osborn Industries sign, and you can hear the bad guys planning their next job. Most guests walk right by this little known secret area.

☐ Find the Fantastic Four™ imprints on the cement

> Before entering the lair of Doctor Doom®, look down at the pavement. The silhouettes of the Fantastic Four®. The Fantastic Four® have fallen from the tower and landed on the cement in front of the entrance to Doctor Doom's Fearfall®.
>
> You can see their outlines on the pavement as you walk through this area.

- ☐ Walk through the lair of Doctor Doom®

    Enter the lair of Doctor Doom® if you are courageous enough. Navigate through the corridors but stop to read the shields before you continue through this dangerous labyrinth.

    Work your way up the ramps as you watch the enormous monitor showing Doctor Doom® at his worst.

- ☐ Ride Doctor Doom Fearfall®

    Strap in to your seat for this thrilling ride as you climb to the highest point of Universal's Islands of Adventure™.

    Unfortunately, you will not be able to enjoy the view for very long before plummeting back to earth at the whim of the evil Doctor Doom®.

- ☐ Get a picture of Dr. Doom's throne

    As you exit your ride, you will come face to face with the throne of Doctor Doom® in the cell, but the evil doctor is nowhere to be found. Has this dastardly villain escaped to create chaos on the streets of Marvel Super Hero Island®?

- ☐ Enjoy arcade games at Kingpin's Arcade®

    Try your hand at some classic arcade games at Kingpin's Arcade® or try a game of skill to win some fabulous prizes but beware; this villain does not play fair.

- ☐ Find the hole made by Johnny Storm® from Café 4®

    Inside Kingpin's Arcade™, you will find a large hole in the wall connecting to Café 4® made by superhero Johnny Storm® to capture Kingpin®.

- ☐ Find Stan Lee Way

    As you exit Kingpin's and arrive back at the corner, look up at the street sign.

    The main street has been named in honor of Marvel artist and Spider-man® creator, Stan Lee.

The Amazing Adventures of Spider-man®

- ☐ Walk through the Daily Planet offices

    Enter the Daily Planet building and get a complete tour of the offices, break room, darkroom, and file room. From the back alley, you will load into your ride, where you will go on an adventure with the web-slinger, Spider-man™.

Notice most of the furnishings and items on the desks are grey to contrast with the brightly colored signs like you are walking through your own comic book.

☐ See the permanent shrine of Stan Lee

Spider-man creator Stan Lee passed away November 12, 2018, in Los Angeles, CA., and fans all over the world mourned the loss of this talented man.

The creators of the Amazing Adventures of Spider-man® created a permanent shrine atop one of the desks, including letters left by the fans. Be sure to spend a moment in tribute to Mr. Lee.

☐ Get a glimpse of the darkroom and file cabinets at the Daily Planet

Guests who walk through the Express queue for the Amazing Adventures of Spider-man® can see a part of the Daily Planet building not accessed through the regular queue.

Guests walk through the darkroom and down a small room housing the file cabinets for the Daily Bugle. Read the labels on the cabinets, and you will find the names of your favorite characters from the Marvel® universe.

Catherine F. Olen

☐ Read the names on the awards housed in the glass cabinets in the queue

> As you walk through the Daily Planet offices, you will come to several glass cases containing the various awards the Daily Planet has won over the years.
>
> If you read the names on these awards, they represent the creators of the attraction you are about to ride.

☐ Ride with Spider-man® and save the city from Doctor Octopus and his gang

> Join Spider-man® as he saves the city from Doctor Octopus and his band of villains. Keep an eye out for his antigravity ray, so you do not end up flying through space.
>
> Try to help the famous crime-fighter, but be sure to keep yourself out of trouble, or you may need Spider-man® to save you too.

☐ Find Stan Lee in the Amazing Adventures of Spider-man®

> As you ride through the city with Spider-man®, you may recognize a familiar character along the way.

Stan can be found several times during your ride. Standing outside the Excelsior Theater, driving the garbage truck, in the crowd during the battle and on the street at the end of your ride. You will also hear Stan's voice as you exit your ride.

☐ Find J. Jonas Jameson at the end of the Amazing Adventures of Spider-man®

As you come to the unload area of The Amazing Adventures of Spider-man®, you will see the anti-gravity gun positioned up to the office of J. Jonah Jameson. The tyrant Jameson is floating high above his desk, a fitting end for Jameson.

☐ Find the Super Villain Ultranet and press the button

As you work your way through Marvel Super Hero Island, you will come to what appears to be several blue speakers. As you approach, press the button, and you will hear the villains planning their next evil plot while the Marvel® superheroes are busily thwarting other evil plans.

☐ Find the meteor crash site on Marvel Super

Along your way through Marvel Super Hero Island®, you will see a large area with four yellow spires and a cloud of dust on the ground. This is the meteor crash site boasting murals of the superheroes it has created, and this area is used for superhero meet and greets.

Check the Universal app to see when your favorite will be appearing throughout the day.

☐ Find the secret entrance to Stark Industries

Towards the rear of the Spider-man® meet and greet, you will find the secret entrance to Stark Industries. Guests would never know this entrance exists, but it is marked once you come to the rear of the building.

☐ Purchase your favorite comic books

Marvel Super Hero Island® is a comic book that comes to life, but you can purchase your favorite superhero comics to take home. Stop in one of the shops and find the newest comic books to take home as souvenirs.

☐ Find Thor's hammer at the Captain America Diner®

As you stand outside the Captain America Diner®, look up at the highest window, and you will see Thor's hammer lodged in the broken window.

Step inside, and you will see the mural of Thor on the opposite wall. Look towards the front windows, and you will see this hammer from the inside.

☐ Dine at the Captain America Diner®

For guests looking for all American fare, stop at the Captain America Diner® for specialty burgers, salads, chicken, or shakes.

There is something for everyone at the Captain America Diner®.

☐ Find the signature of artist Adam Kubert

Throughout Marvel Super Hero Island®, you will see large murals of your favorite comic book superheroes. If you search the detail of these characters, you will notice the artist, Adam Kubert, has signed each book.

Challenge yourself to find his name, sometimes this can be extremely difficult, but the name is there.

Toon Lagoon™

Go back to a simpler time where cartoon animation began. Enjoy seeing some of your all-time favorites while you ride with Popeye, Olive Oyl, Dudley Do-Right, and the rest of the gang.

Adventures await as you join Dudley Do-Right to save Nell from the dastardly Snidely Whiplash. Join Popeye to save Olive Oyl from the mean Bluto.

For guests looking for a bite to eat, try a Dagwood sandwich or eat with your favorite comic strips characters.

☐ Get a picture with the Toon Lagoon™ sign

> As you enter Toon Lagoon™ from Marvel Super Hero Island™, you can get a picture with the Toon Lagoon sign. This is a great photo opportunity for your time in Toon Lagoon™.

- [ ] Try games of skill at Toon Lagoon™ Games

    Along the path to Toon Lagoon™, you will find several booths with games of skill to win adorable characters from your favorite animated films.

    Stop to try your hand at High Strike, Hot Shots, or Bank a Ball and win plush prized from the Minions, the Simpsons or dinosaurs, so step up and try your luck.

- [ ] Explore the comic strips that created the history of animation

    The comic strips you see surrounding you on the buildings in Toon Lagoon™ are from the 1920s and 1930s. These comic strips were created by talented artists each week for the newspapers delivered to millions of homes. These comics were the inspiration to the next generation of animators who read the comic strips and then tried to draw their own characters.

    Each generation built on the animation style of the one before, and today, we have the latest in CGI technology, bringing animation to life.

    Enjoy taking a trip to the origins of animation with these charming comic strips.

☐ Play in the water around the shops of Toon Lagoon™

> While the comic strips are the stars of Toon Lagoon™, the area has another theme, water. As you explore Toon Lagoon™, you will find Hagar bursting through his comic with the water spilling into the red tube below. Nearby, the tube comes out across the walkway to fill the dog filled fountain.
>
> Keep an eye out for surprise water areas throughout Toon Lagoon™.

☐ Find where Broom-Hilda broke through the comic strips

> The witch Broom-Hilda has broken through the comic strip entrance to the Comic Strip Café™ and has crashed into the lamppost. Listen as you check out her crash site, and you can hear her complain about her nose hurting.
>
> Poor Broom-Hilda is even showing off her U.S.M.C. undies.

☐ Pose for a picture with Spikes doghouse from the comic strip Heathcliff®

> Spike's purple doghouse is standing near the Comic Strip Café™ with Heathcliff® sitting above

dangling a juicy bone to lure Spike out to torment him.

Now you can pose for an amusing picture with this great backdrop for your photo album.

☐ Grab a bite to eat at the Comic Strip Café™

Step inside the Comic Strip Café™ and get a hearty meal while you sit among classic comic strips. Read the comics while you eat, and you will find yourself giggling throughout your meal.

Check out the backside of the lockers to see items from the Cat in the Hat® and even see Woody Woodpecker inside one of the lockers.

☐ Try the jackhammer at Aesop and Son

The famous storyteller Aesop and his son can be found on the patio of the Comic Strip Café™. These animated cartoons were part of the Rocky and Bullwinkle television show with Aesop's son using a jackhammer to carve the marble instead of using the traditional chisel like his father.

Now you can try the jackhammer for yourself on the patio. Be sure to pose for great pictures with these two famous figures before you go on with your day.

- [ ] Follow the dotted line path from the Family Circus comic

    Find the Family Circus comic, one panel about an American family. Notice the dotted line that follows Billy's path beginning inside the panel. This dotted line trails around Toon Lagoon™ and ends at another comic.

    Follow the line to see where Billy went and what the note read.

- [ ] Listen to Betty Boop sing

    Standing above the walkway, you will find Betty Boop sitting atop her piano at the entrance to her shop. If you stand below and listen, you can hear Betty Boop singing her famous song; *Boo oop a Doop*.

- [ ] Stop in at the Betty Boop Store

    Betty Boop sits high above Toon Lagoon®, sitting atop her piano. Step into her signature store and find your favorite Betty Boop merchandise to take home.

    Everything from clothing to purses to jewelry can be found inside. There is something for everyone at the Betty Boop store.

☐ Get a Dagwood Sandwich at Blondies

> The comic strip Blondie was famous for the sandwich her husband Dagwood makes for himself. Now you can get the famous Dagwood for yourself at Blondie at Toon Lagoon™.
>
> Stop in to order this signature sandwich and see what the fuss is all about.

☐ Grab an ice cream at Cathy's Ice Cream

> Step up to Cathy's Ice Cream for a delicious treat with one, two, or three scoops with all the toppings or an ice-cold shake to cool off on a hot day.
>
> Cathy is diving into a yummy treat high above her shop but walks to the side of her sign to see the diving board she has jumped off.

☐ Pose for a picture with the speech balloons

> Throughout Toon Lagoon™, you will find speech balloons with witty sayings. Find your favorite and position yourself for the perfect picture to send to your friends or post on social media.

- ☐ Pose for a picture with the sinking rowboat

    Find the rowboat that has been snapped in two and jump in before it sinks for a cute picture with the characters from the comic strip Pogo.

    Get creative with this cute picture opportunity before it sinks.

- ☐ Check out the gang from the comic strip Tumbleweeds®

    Find the frontier community of Tumbleweeds®, most of the townspeople are atop the cactus to get away from an ornery skunk while the town undertaker is waiting patiently for his next client.

    This is a great area to get creative with your vacation photos, so have fun while posing with these cute characters.

- ☐ Find your favorite characters in Toon Extra™

    Your favorite characters have jumped right off the pages of the comics and into this delightful store.

    Throughout Toon Extra™, you will find everything from clothing, plush toys, mugs, and toys to take home. Be sure to spend lots of time looking through the shelves as you wander through this awesome store.

☐ Check out the pillar of newspapers inside Toon Extra™

> Within Toon Extra™, one of the pillars is not like the others. Find the large stack of newspapers with the comic section facing you.
>
> This is just another example of the amazing attention to detail throughout this charming island.

☐ Pose for pictures with Beetle Baily

> Outside Toon Extra™ is private Beetle Bailey lounging next to his camouflage tent. Stand inside just below the light bulb for a great picture.
>
> Be sure to look down at the ground before you move on to see his tent camouflage has bled onto the surrounding walkway.

☐ Get a picture of the Popeye the Sailor® statue

> Standing above the planter in the center of Toon Lagoon™ stands the most iconic sailor in animation, Popeye the Sailor®. This bronze statue shows Popeye® at the wheel of his ship.
>
> Be sure to get a picture of this famous sailor next time you walk through Toon Lagoon™.

☐ Grab a bite at Wimpy's

> Popeye's old friend Wimpy has finally gotten his own Hamburger emporium, so he does not have to ask for a hamburger from his friends. Step up for a classic Wimpy burger, but be sure to have your money since he probably will not let you pay on Tuesday.

Popeye & Bluto's Bilge-rat Barges

☐ Read the notices in the queue for Popeye & Bluto's Bilge-rat Barges®

> As you walk through the queue for Popeye and Bluto's Bilge-rat Barges®, be sure to spend some time reading the notices for the activities during your cruise.

> Be sure to check out the cruise schedule before you head towards Bluto's office. Be sure not to pull the rope, or you may be in for a big surprise.

> As you arrive on the dock, the fun is just beginning

☐ Check out Bluto's office in the queue for Popeye & Bluto's Bilge-rat Barges®

> There is no doubt which office is occupied by Bluto, the dastard character. The huge hole in the

wall and the poor parrot hanging from the wall are just a few of the crazy décor in the office, so check it out as you walk by.

☐ Get wet and save Olive Oyl on Popeye &Bluto's Bilge-rat Barges®

Board your boat and get ready for a wide ride through the rapids as you help Popeye save his girl, Olive Oyl, from the bully Bluto. Find the baby Sweet Pea along the way and hold on tight as you traverse the rapids that will soak you to the bone.

☐ Visit Popeye's boat The Olive

Wander close to the water and climb aboard Popeye's boat, The Olive. Climb the rigging and work your way to the captain's quarters.

Be sure to play the piano while you can. You may recognize the tune on the sheet music sitting on the keyboard.

☐ Walk down by the water at Toon Lagoon™

If you follow the path behind the Olive, you can walk around the water's edge and find some fun toon related gags.

Find the school of fish, and the dotted line to the X marks the spot. Lastly, come to the mailboxes for Popeye, Sweet Pea, and Wimpy along the way.

☐ Step into Gasoline Alley

Step inside the service station for Gasoline Alley and find another great store with toon themed merchandise.

Listen carefully, and you will hear old time radio shows being played inside this shop.

☐ Find the leaky tire outside Gasoline Alley

Outside the Gasoline Alley store, you will find a stack of old tires in need of repairs. If you walk towards the back of these tires and listen, you will take notice of one leaking air.

This may make it difficult to sell these tires.

☐ Pose for a picture with Marmaduke

Along the path, you will find a comic strip panel that seems to be positioned in the wrong way. The Great Dane, Marmaduke, is running straight up in the air with the leash hanging down behind him, but this comic strip set up this way on purpose.

Step up to the panel and hold onto the leash while your photographer turns the camera, so it appears you are being dragged behind the dog as he runs away with you.

☐ Try the plunger on the Hush A-Bomb

On the path in front of the Wossamotta-U store, stands a comically large red bomb. If you look to the side of this bomb, you will find a metal plunger waiting for someone to step up and give it a try.

You may surprise the guests standing nearby when the bomb explodes.

☐ Visit Wossamotta-U

Fans of the Rocky and Bullwinkle show know that Bullwinkle Moose graduated from Wossamotta-U, and now you can enter this famous college to do some shopping.

Find not only animation souvenirs but great clothing items just in case you get soaked on one of the water rides in Toon Lagoon®.

Dudley Do-Right's Ripsaw Falls®

☐ Find the heads carved in the mountain of Dudley Do-Right's Ripsaw Falls®

> High above the rest of Universal's Islands of Adventure™ stands the mountain of Dudley Do-Rights Ripsaw Falls® and the four main characters that have been carved into this mountain. Here you will find Dudley, Nell, Horse, and Nell's father, the commander.
>
> This enormous façade hints at the excitement that awaits you when you traverse the mountain for yourself.

☐ Walk through the backstage at Dudley Do-Rights Ripsaw Falls®

> As you enter the mountain, you will find yourself at the ticket booth and popcorn concessions, but there is never anyone there to help you.
>
> Walk through the mine and keep an eye out for the canary to make sure there is plenty of air before heading backstage and past the dressing rooms of our stars.
>
> Explore the props and scenery in the backstage area before boarding your log to star in your own melodrama.

- [ ] Watch the cartoons in the load area for Dudley Do-Right's Ripsaw Falls®

    As you wait in the loading area for your ride, be sure to watch the large screen above for the latest melodrama to flicker across the screen.

    These hilarious cartoons are classic examples of the early days of cartoon animation.

- [ ] Save Nell from Snidely Whiplash on Dudley Do-Rights Ripsaw Falls®

    Board your log and begin your journey to boo the villain and cheer the bumbling hero as you follow in the steps of Dudley as he attempts to rescue Nell with the help of his horse.

    Keep an eye out for the dastardly Snidely Whiplash as he tries to stay one step ahead of our hero.

    Hold on for your dear life as you plunge from the top of the mountain on this wild ride.

- [ ] Get the riders soaked with the water cannons at Dudley Do-Rights Ripsaw Falls®

    Unsuspecting riders will never see the sneak attack from the guests on the bridge, but you can be one of them as you pay your money to aim the water cannons at the riders below.

Aim just right, and you will soak the riders from head to toe.

Skull Island: Reign of Kong

Go on an adventure to a strange island where time stands still. Do you have the courage to come face to face with the greatest beast known to man? Find out on Skull Island.

☐ Take the behind the scenes tour of the temple

> Guests wanting an in-depth look at the temple at Reign of Kong can ask the guides at the entrance for a guided tour.
>
> While the tour is not always available, you usually can find them available if you arrive early in the morning or late in the afternoon, so do not miss this great opportunity to see the secrets of the temple for yourself.

☐ Walk through the temple on Skull Island: Reign on Kong

> The queue for Skull Island: Reign of Kong takes you through an ancient temple that has been discovered deep in the jungle of Skull Island. Walk

through the gates and go on an adventure that leads you through narrow passageways and temple rooms.

Keep your wits about you, or you may fall victim to ambush from the natives lurking in the darkness.

☐ Get a picture with the Shaman in the temple at Skull Island: Reign of King

As you enter the main temple, you will come to a large room with the shaman chanting to bring the temple to life. Stop for a moment to pose for a unique picture with this ancient shaman.

☐ Get a picture of the giant worm in the queue

As you get closer to the loading area, you will find a large plexiglass case with an enormous worm-like creature. As you watch this creature, you will see it wiggle beneath the glass.

☐ Survive a dinosaur attack with King Kong

Step aboard a transport vehicle and trust your driver to get you to the encampment safely as you enter the temple of Kong.

Witness the gigantic bat creatures and the dinosaurs that man assumed extinct before coming face to face with Kong. Be sure to ride this attraction more than once to ride along with a different driver for a slightly different adventure.

Jurassic Park

Explore a world where dinosaurs roam free among the guests of Islands of Adventure. Get up close and personal with the experts or ride down the river to see history come alive right before your eyes.

For the truly brave, meet one of the deadliest dinosaurs that have ever walked the earth face to face.

Join the scientists as they breed a new generation of dinosaurs. Be there to watch a newly hatched dinosaur and maybe even pet a baby dinosaur.

- [ ] Find the fossils in the path at Jurassic Park

    As you walk along the path at Jurassic Park, look down at the ground, and you will see the imprints of plant and animal fossils. This is your first hint to the world that you are entering, a world that once thrived, but now is a memory.

☐ Walk through the caverns at Camp Jurassic

> The Camp Jurassic area is a wonderful place where children can explore the world around them. Hidden in the back corner of this area is a series of caverns where you can find fossilize amber waiting to be discovered.
>
> Watch out for the hot springs, or you may get wet before you are done.

☐ Step on the dinosaur footprints for a surprise

> Along the path inside Camp Jurassic, you will come to several dinosaur footprints. You will get a very big surprise when you hear dinosaurs roaring around you as you put your foot in the footprints.

☐ Ride the Pteranodon Flyers

> One attraction at Camp Jurassic is designed just for the kids. The Pteranodon Flyers let families with children get a bird's eye view of the Camp Jurassic area while experiencing what it was like to be one of these winged dinosaurs.

☐ Find a hearty meal at Thunder Falls Terrace™

> For guests looking for an amazing meal, try Thunder Falls Terrace™ in Jurassic Park. Try

the Ribs or an Angus burger to keep you going during your day.

Sit in comfort while you enjoy your meal and take a rest before continuing your day.

☐ Ride the Jurassic Park River Adventure

The signature attraction of Jurassic Park is the Jurassic Park River Adventure, a water attraction that allows guests to get up close with several docile species of dinosaur.

Your adventure will let you come close to several species of a carnivore, but not to worry; these dinosaurs are under control. Your river cruise will come to the finale, an eighty-five-foot drop back to the unload area where you will get soaked.

☐ Try your hand at the carnival games in Jurassic Park

Take home a great souvenir of your time at Jurassic Park while trying your hand on old fashion carnival games.

Step up to your favorite games and find Jurassic Park themed merchandise you cannot get in the stores.

☐ Visit the Jurassic Park Dinosaur Institute

> Within the Jurassic Park Dinosaur Institute, you will find the past and present come together with fossils and live dinosaurs. Watch as a baby dinosaur hatches right before your eyes then explore the dioramas with full dinosaur fossils and dinosaur statues.
>
> Learn the origins of dinosaurs and explore the interactive exhibits to come to a new understanding of these magnificent creatures.

☐ See a baby dinosaur hatch

> Within the hatchery, you will get the chance to see a baby Velociraptor hatch in the incubator. The Jurassic Park scientists are on hand to explain the procedure and give you facts about the species we have come to know more intimately within the institute.
>
> If you are a lucky guest, you can even name the new baby and get a certificate to take home as a souvenir.

☐ Interact with dinosaur eggs and see what is inside

> Step up to the interactive x-ray machines and place the dinosaur egg inside to see what species are waiting to hatch. Use the CT Scan to see the

details of the development of the dinosaur species before they hatch.

- [ ] Get a tour of the baby dinosaur lab

    Periodically, guests can be invited into the lab behind the glass to interact with the scientist and learn more about how the Jurassic Park Dinosaur Institute runs.

    While this private tour is not available most of the time, you may be one of a lucky few to receive the royal treatment.

- [ ] Find the Barbasol can with the false compartment inside the lab

    Fans of the *Jurassic Park* film remember the evil Nedry stealing the dinosaur embryos from the lab in the can of Barbasol shaving cream, and this can is sitting on one of the shelves within the lab.

    Spend some time looking for this Easter egg from this famous film.

- [ ] Pet a baby dinosaur

    The scientists will hold special talks for the guests of the Jurassic Park Dinosaur Institute and bring a baby dinosaur out for the guests to interact with.

You can pet these docile creatures, and the handlers will explain the growth process and how these babies are raised in Jurassic Park.

☐ Get up close with a Raptor at the Raptor Encounter

Guest who is brave enough can come face to face with one of the most ferocious predators to ever walk the Earth. The Raptor Encounter experts explain the behavior of the Velociraptors before bringing the animal out to pose for pictures but heed their warnings, or you could be the next meal.

The Wizarding World of Harry Potter™ - Hogsmeade™

As you enter the magical, mystical world of Harry Potter, you will explore the well-known shops and attractions that bring you right to the heart of the Harry Potter™ books. Become a wizard yourself when you don your robes, hold your wand in hand, and transport yourself to a world where anything is possible.

Fly on a broom as you explore Hogwarts™ Castle or meet a Hippogriff on an exciting rollercoaster.

Join Hagrid as you explore the magical creatures that are his best friends. Be sure to visit the wand master at Ollivanders™ to get your new wand before your time in Hogsmeade™ is through.

☐ Cross the Bridge to Hogsmeade

> If you cross the bridge from the Jurassic Park area to the Wizarding World of Harry Potter™ -

Hogsmeade™ over the wooden bridge, the view that awaits you is nothing short of spectacular.

As you cross the bridge, the façade of Hogwarts™ Castle is the first view that greets you building the excitement that awaits you in Hogsmeade™.

Harry Potter and the Forbidden Journey™

☐ Walk through Hogwarts™ School of Witchcraft and Wizardry

Enter the dungeon of Hogwarts™, and your journey begins as you work your way through the corridors and into the castle itself.

Walk the very same halls as your favorite characters in the Harry Potter series of books and keep an eye out for the characters as you will come face to face with them along the way.

☐ Find Mr. Weasley's enchanted car

As you work your way through the outer queue before entering the castle, you will find Mr. Weasley's car parked outside. Listen as the car attempts to come to life again.

Get some very creative pictures with this famous car as you pass by.

☐ Stare into the Mirror of Erised

> One of the first things you come in contact with in the dungeon will be the Mirror of Erised. Fans of the Harry Potter books know this mirror shows the observer their heart's desire. Keep moving, or you may not be able to look away.

☐ Listen to Neville as he is tutored in the Potions classroom

> Neville is busy with extra tutoring in the potions classroom, and you can stand outside the door of this classroom and eavesdrop on the conversation. If you listen carefully, you will hear him working hard at his studies.

☐ Find the house points within Hogwarts™ castle

> As you come through the herbology area and back into the castle, you will find house points for the four houses of Hogwarts™.
>
> It would appear that Gryffindor is currently ahead for the school year.

☐ Examine the statue of the Hogwarts™ architect

> Standing just inside the main entrance to the castle, you will find a golden statue of the architect

of Hogwarts™. If you examine the statue carefully, you will find the four mascots of the four houses at his feet.

☐ Find the secret entrance to Head Master Dumbledore's office

As you work your way through the corridor, you will come to a large statue before the corridor curves to the left. This statue hides the entrance to the Head Master's office.

☐ Listen to the paintings that chat with you

The painting hall of Hogwarts™ has dozens of animated portraits that are excited to greet you and have a chat. Listen carefully to these famous witches and wizards as they may reveal the secrets of Hogwarts™.

☐ Listen to the heads of the houses bicker in their paintings

The four wizards that make up the founders of Hogwarts™ still cannot seem to get along as they bicker back and forth about the state of the school and whether muggles should be allowed within the castle walls.

☐ Find the Pensieve within Dumbledore's office

> The metal Pensieve sits by the shelves in Dumbledore's office. Fans of the Harry Potter books know this Pensieve is used to see the memories that have been captured when poured out into the water within the basin.

☐ Listen to Professor Dumbledore in his office

> As you enter the Head Master's office, you will be greeted by Dumbledore himself. Listen intently as he gives you a solemn warning about your future and talks about the Defense Against the Dark Arts classroom and the history of Hogwarts™.

☐ Find Harry, Hermione, and Ron in the Defense Against the Dark Arts Classroom

> As you enter the dimly lit Defense Against the Dark Arts classroom, you may hear voices without seeing the individuals. Suddenly, you will come face to face with Ron, Hermione, and Harry as they tell you about the school and invite you to watch a Quidditch™ match.

☐ Read the blackboard in the Defense Against the Dark Arts classroom

> At the front of the classroom, you will find an old-fashioned blackboard with instructions on how to repel a Dementor.
>
> Read the instructions as you pass by so you will be able to control these dark figures.

☐ Find a secret entrance to the Gryffindor common room

> As you exit the Defense Against the Dark Arts classroom, do not walk too quickly down the hall. The life-size painting sitting quietly in the hall will suddenly come to life and cheer for her favorite Quidditch™ team.
>
> Cheer along with her as you work your way through the castle.

☐ Listen to the sorting hat

> As you get closer to your ride with Harry Potter, you will find the famous sorting hat. Listen as the hat gives you instructions for the ride you are about to embark on.
>
> Make sure you are taller than a goblin to ride this attraction.

☐ Ride with Harry and Ron in the Harry Potter and the Forbidden Journey™

> Step into your vehicle and let Hermione create the magic to let you fly with Ron and Harry. Keep up with them as you explore the castle landscape before being chased by dangerous creatures and dementors.
>
> Play a game of Quidditch™ before taking a trip to the bowels of the castle. Watch out for Dementors, Dragons, and Spiders as you try to make it back alive.

☐ Explore Filch's Emporium of Confiscated Goods for confiscated student items

> Mr. Filch has been busy taking possessions from the Hogwarts™ students, and you can find the boxes labeled with the names of your favorite characters throughout this shop.
>
> Sitting atop the many shelves, you will find nondescript boxes keeping his treasures organized. For other items, he has shoved them into the beams above your head. Within these hollow beams, you will find fireworks, gags, and many other items that will never be returned to their owners.

☐ Find your new Hogwarts™ souvenir within Filch's Emporium of Confiscated Goods

> Everything you could need for a year at Hogwarts™ can be found within Filch's Emporium of Confiscated Goods. Shop by your house colors or pick out your new pet from the various plush pets on the shelves.
>
> Find detailed collectibles and Christmas items within this shop as you exit the castle.

☐ See the Nighttime Lights at Hogwarts™ Castle

> Each evening, after the sun goes down, Hogwarts™ Castle comes to life and lights up the night sky. The castle honors each house and shows the magic of this historic school.
>
> Be sure to include this stunning visual event during your day at Hogsmeade™.

Flight of the Hippogriff™

☐ Walk through Hagrid's garden

> As you work your way through the queue for Flight of the Hippogriff™, you will come to Hagrid's garden full of ripe pumpkins. Be sure to notice his scarecrow is wearing official

Hogwarts's™ robes to scare away pests trying to eat his garden.

☐ Listen to the conversation within Hagrid's hut

As you walk past Hagrid's hut, you will hear a heated conversation within. Eavesdrop on the conversation as you walk by, and you may hear Fang barking also.

☐ Find Hagrid's motorbike outside his hut

Parked outside Hagrid's hut is his favorite motorbike. Hagrid uses this to travel through the wizarding and muggle worlds across the sky.

Fans of the Harry Potter books know this bike was given to Hagrid by Sirius Black, the bikes first owner.

☐ Ride Flight of the Hippogriff™

Step in the ride car and take off on this fun rollercoaster. Wave at the baby Hippogriff™ as you begin your adventure that takes you up hills and down on this rollercoaster fit for the whole family.

☐ Enjoy the songs of the Frog Choir

The students of Hogwarts™ take to the stage with their frogs to sing for the guests of Hogsmeade™.

Make time to see these talented students in their show on the outdoor stage during your time in the Wizarding World of Harry Potter™.

☐ Meet the visiting students at the Triwizard Spirit Rally

The students from Durmstrang and Beauxbatons are visiting Hogwarts™ to compete in the Triwizard tournament, and you have a chance to see the spirit rally on the outdoor stage in Hogsmeade™.

Ollivanders™

☐ Attend a wand fitting at Ollivanders™

Every new wizard dreams of getting their wand fitting at Ollivanders™, and now you have your chance to be selected by the wand master during the Ollivanders™ wand fitting demonstration.

The wand master will select a young student and find the perfect wand to fit the newest wizard.

☐ Walk through the wand displays at Ollivanders™

Find your perfect wand at Ollivanders™ after you have finished the wand fitting demonstration. Whether you are looking for the wand of your favorite Harry Potter character or a custom wand of your own, you will find the perfect wand to take home with you.

The shelves are lined with thousands of wands in every shape and color, so take your time to let the perfect wand pick you.

☐ Taste a Butterbeer™

Fans of the Wizarding World of Harry Potter™ now have the chance to drink the signature drink they have read about in their favorite Harry Potter books.

Step up to the cart on the street and order a Butterbeer™; this butterscotch flavored drink is enjoyed by millions of visitors.

Take home a souvenir by ordering your Butterbeer™ in a souvenir mug.

☐ Look in the window of Tomes and Scrolls Specialty Bookshop

Stand in front of Tomes and Scrolls Specialty Bookshop and see what new books are being sold by this fictitious bookseller.

The writer Gilderoy Lockhart has been busy writing his books, as you can see by the display in the window.

☐ Watch the Tales of Beedle Bard come to life

Guests with interactive wands can cast a spell to open the Tales of Beedle Bard and see what lays beneath the cover. You can attempt this spell or watch as others create this magic.

☐ Visit the conveniences and listen to Moaning Myrtle

Step inside the conveniences, known as restrooms in the muggle world, and hear the voice of Moaning Myrtle as she converses with you.

This famous ghost will whine about her day or poke fun as you take care of your business.

The Owl Post™

☐ Visit the Owl Post

Step inside the Owl Post™ to get all of your stationery needs. Whether you are looking for stationary, quills, stamps, or postcards, you will find everything within the Owl Post™.

Examine the stacks of packages waiting for the owls to deliver to their new owners before looking above at the owls resting before they head out again.

☐ Listen to the howler outside the Owl Post™

Step outside the owl post and look at the window between the packages. Suddenly a howler will appear and yell at you about a variety of infractions. Be sure to spend time watching the howlers to get all of your messages before moving on.

Dervish and Banges™

☐ Find the Monster Book of Monsters in Dervish and Banges™

Step into Dervish and Banges and find the Monster Book of Monster sitting in the center of the room in a cage.

This sleeping book may just wake up and try to attack the guests looking, so be careful and do not stick your fingers in the cage.

☐ Find the brooms tethered within Dervish and Banges™

High above the first floor, you will see three brooms tethered to the second-floor rail. Watch them as they sway in the air waiting for their owners to return.

☐ Read the closing instructions in Dervish and Banges™

Behind the counter of Dervish and Banges™, you will find the closing instructions for the staff to follow each evening.

Read the numbered list, and you will see how detailed the closing of this wizarding shop can be for the staff.

☐ Find the model of Hogwarts™ in the window of Dervish and Banges™

Outside Dervish and Banges™, you will find a detailed model of Hogwarts™ castle. If you wave your interactive wand, you can bring the dragon to life to chase the poor Quidditch™ player.

Gladrags Wizardwear™

☐ Purchase your own robes in Gladrags Wizardwear™

New students in Hogwarts™ can step into Gladrags Wizardwear™ and find the perfect size. Within this specialty store, you can also find scarves, ties, and accessories to complete your ensemble.

☐ Find the sweater given to Ron and Harry by Mrs. Weasley

> Inside Gladrags Wizardwear™, you will find an item that is not sold anywhere else in Hogsmeade™.
>
> Gladrags sells the sweater given to Ron and Harry by Mrs. Weasley *in Harry Potter and the Sorcerer's Stone*. These wool sweaters can now be yours to wear on a chilly Christmas morning, just like Ron and Harry.

☐ Admire the Yule Ball gowns within Gladrags Wizardwear™

> Fans of the Harry Potter films will recognize the gowns hanging on the mannequins within this shop. Hermione's pink gown can be purchased, but the other gowns are one of a kind and not available for purchase.

Hogs Head™

☐ Visit the Hogs Head™

> Step inside this small bar inside Hogsmeade™ for a cold Butterbeer™ or something little harder. Try a specialty ale or pumpkin juice as you enjoy the coolness of the Hogs Head™.

☐ Watch the Hogs Head move and snort

> Mounted behind the bar is a large hogs head which gave this bar its name. Watch as the head moves from side to side and snorts his displeasure then falls silent.

☐ Listen to the house-elves on the second floor of the Hogs Head™

> Walk to the base of the stairs to the left of the bar and listen to the activity on the second floor. Upstairs you can hear house elves working hard to keep the rooms clean and care for the weary travelers.

The Three Broomsticks™

☐ Get a bite to eat at the Three Broomsticks™

> Inside the Three Broomsticks™, you will find wonderful dishes from the UK. Try Fish and Chips, Shepherd's Pie or Beef Pasties to keep you going on a long day.
>
> For groups looking for a sumptuous meal, try the Feast, a complete meal for four, one of the best food values throughout the theme park.

☐ Look for house-elves shadows

As you sit inside the Three Broomsticks™ enjoying your meal, you may catch a glimpse of shadows on the walls that quickly fade away. These are shadows of the house-elves working on the second floor, so keep your eyes peeled for this elusive detail.

Honeydukes™

☐ Visit Honeydukes™ for something sweet

Within Honeydukes™, you will find a world of sweets for any taste. The shelves are lined with chocolates in the shape of frogs, cauldrons, and wands, as well as Pink Ice and Sugar Skulls like the ones you have seen in the Harry Potter films.

Inside the case, you will find Pumpkin Pasties and No Melt Ice Cream on the shelves lined with yummy pastries. Be sure to sample your favorites while inside Honeydukes™.

☐ Watch the Eyeball Bonanza in the window of Honeydukes™

The Eyeball Bonanza machine in the window of Honeydukes™ comes to life every few seconds as the skull tips his hat to reveal a raven who plucks his eye out. Watch closely as the eyeball appears in the slot below.

☐ Watch the Wizards Chessboard in the window of Zonko's

> The display for Wizards Chess shows how violent this form of chess can be as the pieces move closer together, and one breaks apart in the battle.
>
> A favorite game of Ron and Harry, this display of Wizards Chess is another great detail from the wizarding world.

☐ Find the pixie outside Zonko's

> Outside Zonko's, you will find a cauldron waiting for new wizards to cast a spell revealing a pixie. If wizards cast the spell just right, the cauldron tips forward, and the little pixie giggles at you.

Hagrid's Magical Creatures Motorbike Adventure™

☐ Check out the Blast-ended Skrewt's pumpkin patch

> As you work your way through the queue for Hagrid's Magical Creatures Motorbike Adventure™, you will come to the Blast-ended Skrewt's shack with his garden full of ripe pump-

kins. These creatures were cared for by Hagrid against the Ministry of Magic wishes, and now you can see how they live.

Wonder at the process of getting these gourds to grow to their enormous sizes as you walk by.

☐ Find the mermaid in stone outside the castle ruins

Just before you enter the ruins, you will find an archway with a mermaid in stone. These dangerous creatures are known to terrorize anyone brave enough to swim in the lake inhabited by them, so be thankful you are seeing an artist's rendering of this creature.

☐ Find the magical creature graffiti

Someone has been busy drawing magical creatures on the walls of these ruins. You will come through a small room inside the castle ruins, so take some time to admire the artistry before continuing your exploration.

☐ Watch Hagrid and Mr. Weasley get the motorbikes ready for you

Along your path through the ruins, you will find Hagrid and Mr. Weasley working on Hagrid's motorbike to get it ready for your adventure.

Watch as the mischievous Cornish Pixies cause chaos for the two men.

☐ Watch Hagrid's motorbikes take off and land on the rooftop

As you come to another large room in the queue, look up at the ceiling, and you will see the motorbikes taking off and landing in a chaotic frenzy. These enchanted motorbikes seem to be quite busy based on the activity going on.

☐ Ride Hagrid's Magical Creatures Motorbike Adventure™

Step aboard your motorbike and get ready for the ride of a lifetime. Dash through the dark forest and come across the elusive magical creatures Hagrid cares for. Watch out for danger around every corner before you come back to the safety of the ruins from where you came.

☐ Ride the Hogwarts Express™ from Hogsmeade™ to Kings Cross Station

Walkthrough the train station in Hogsmeade™ and get ready to ride the HogwartsExpress™ to London. In your private train car, you can look out the window at the countryside and see Centaurs running alongside the train tracks before seeing the Weasley twins having fun.

Keep an eye out for Mad-Eye Moody™ and the Knight Bus as you come through London and back to the land of the muggles.

☐ Find the carriage pulled by the Thestral™ at Hogsmeade™ Station

As you exit the Hogwarts Express™ in Hogsmeade™, you will walk by a black carriage that seems to move back and forth on its own power.

Fans of the Harry Potter books know that this carriage is being powered by an invisible mythical creature known as the Thestral™ with a skeletal body and wings.

The Lost Continent

Travel to a world of ancient myths when you arrive on the Lost Continent. Travel from the world of Sinbad, where ancient tales come to life or travel to a world from beneath the sea when you explore the ruins of the temple of Poseidon.

This land offers adventure along with enchanting souvenirs to take home with you to remember the time spent in the Lost Continent.

☐ Have a chat with the Mystic Fountain

> As you walk along the shop stalls in the Lost Continent, you will come to an ornate fountain, but this fountain is unlike any other.
>
> Say Hello, and this fountain may just say hello back. Ask the oracle questions about love, money, or your future, and it will share secrets of your life, but be careful, if you upset the oracle, you may come out soaking wet.

☐ Try a kebab at Doc Sugrue's Desert Kebab House

> Guests looking for something to eat during their exploration of the Lost Continent can grab a kebab at the Doc Sugrue's Desert Kebab House near the Mystic Fountain.
>
> These delicacies from the far east in chicken, beef, or vegetable will satisfy your hunger on the long trail. Sides include hummus, yogurt, and fresh fruit to bring the tastes of the far east to Orlando.

☐ Taste a savory Gyros at Fire Eaters Grill™

> The perfect grab and go food, a Gyros is a hearty fare for your time in the Lost Continent. Guests can find their favorite flavors or try something new at this enchanting food stall in the Lost Continent.

☐ Explore the Shop of Wonders

> One of the more unique shops at Universal's Islands of Adventure can be found in the Lost Continent. Step through the doors of Shop of Wonders and find one of a kind works of art from around the world, as well as clothing, collectibles, and jewelry.
>
> In every corner of Shop of Wonders, you will find something that will pique your curiosity, so be

☐ Find one of a kind jewelry at Mythical Metals

> The artisans working within Mythical Metals will take you back in time when they create coin medallions right before your eyes with a technique invented by Leonardo DaVinci.
>
> Select the coin, and the artist will place it in the press with the design you select and watch as they apply fifty pounds of pressure to create dazzling jewelry.
>
> These spectacular medallions are a fantastic souvenir to make you the envy of others when they see your new jewelry.

☐ Have your fortune told at Star Souls – Psychic Readings

> For guests wondering what the future holds for them, step into the tent for Star Souls and have your fortune told by the psychic in residence. Ask your questions or let the psychic read for you and let the stars decide what you need to know.
>
> Either way, you will have fun with this exceptional theme park experience.

☐ Shop in the Treasures of Poseidon

> Step inside Treasures of Poseidon to find lovely clothing perfect for the Florida weather. Beachwear, dresses, and shirts will make you feel cool and fashionable.
>
> Be sure to look in the jewelry cases for ocean-inspired items that will complete your ensemble.

☐ Find the Merman sculpture

> A bronze merman is holding the sign for Treasures of Poseidon, but this sculpture is truly unique. If you look carefully, you will notice this sculpture goes through the building with the tail found on the inside of the shop.

☐ Have an elegant dinner at Mythos

> Enter the ancient rock formation for a one of a kind dining experience. Mythos offers a sumptuous meal in a stunning restaurant with sculptures surrounding you.
>
> Enjoy salads, burgers, Thai food, and more as you sit adjacent to a flowing waterfall within Mythos.

☐ Experience the Temple of Poseidon

> As you walk through the Lost Continent, you will come to the ruins of an ancient temple to the Greek God, Poseidon. Outside, you will find pieces of a broken statue with the hand of Poseidon still holding his trident.
>
> Walk down the path to enormous doors and walk into the darkened corridors to work your way to the archeological dig to discover the wonders of this temple.

☐ Experience Poseidon's Fury

> This often-overlooked attraction offers guests a chance to explore an ancient temple with your guide. Go deep into the temple to see the treasures long since forgotten by an extinct civilization, but beware; you may awaken the ghosts of the Greek Gods.
>
> This walk-through attraction exposes guests to many special effects and darkened tunnels lasting almost thirty minutes.
>
> This is a must-see for anyone that comes through the Lost Continent.

☐ Pick a pearl at the Pearl Factory

> Walk up to the counter of the Pearl Factory, and you can select an oyster from the tank to find a treasure within. The pearl expert will open and clean your new treasure, then measure the pearl and show you the color on the color scale.
>
> Once you have your new pearl, you have the chance to select a setting from a variety of pendants and earrings.

☐ Listen for the ogre that lives under the bridge

> At the water's edge near the Mythos Restaurant, you will find a small wooden bridge. If you listen as you cross the bridge, you may hear the troll that lives beneath growling, so move quickly before you become his next victim.

Seuss Landing™

See the world of Dr. Seuss come to life in this whimsical world where you will find your favorite characters have come to life. Travel with the Cat in the Hat™ or The Sneetches™ as you explore this adorable world where parents and kids can have fun together.

Become the main character in your favorite stories when you fall in love with Dr. Seuss all over again.

☐ Read both sides of the Seuss Landing sign

> As you enter Seuss Landing from the Lost Continent, you will come to the crooked sign welcoming you to this enchanting area. Look up at the opposite side of this sign as you walk beneath and read the clever poem that offers a farewell to guests leaving towards the Lost Continent.

☐ Find the Zamp in the Lamp

> One of the first references to the world of Dr. Seuss is the lamppost with a sign "The Zamp in

the Lamp." During the day, you can make out the silhouette within the frosted glass, but the Zamp can be seen clearly in the evening, so look up to find this little character.

☐ Get a cold drink at Moose Juice Goose Juice

Step up to get an ice-cold Moose Juice or Goose Juice to keep you cool on a hot day. Just like the story of Moose and Goose, you can choose from your favorite flavor along with a snack to keep you going as you navigate Seuss Landing™.

☐ Find your favorite sweets at Snooker and Snooker Sweet Candy Cookers

Guests looking for something sweet, look no further than Snooker and Snooker Sweet Candy Cookers. This shop holds your favorite bulk candy, as well as yummy fudge and candy apples.

Step up to the counter to get your favorite snack as you continue your way through Seuss Landing™.

☐ Find your Dr. Seuss souvenirs at Mulberry Street™ Store

As you peruse the shelves of Mulberry Street™ Store, you will find everything you could want from the world of Dr. Seuss. Find the Cat in the

Hat™ or the Grinch™ merchandise within this adorable store.

Whether you are looking for clothing, toys, or collectibles, you will find a new favorite within Mulberry Street™ Store.

☐ Listen to the Who's Asleep score in the small doorway

As you stand in front of the entrance to Mulberry Street™ Store, you will see a smaller doorway made just for the kids. If you enter through this doorway, you will hear the resounding snore of the Who's Asleep Score.

☐ Find the giraffes from the story *And to Think I Saw it on Mulberry Street*

Fans of the story, *And to Think I Saw it on Mulberry Street,* will find the two giraffes on the roof of the Mulberry Street™ Store.

These Giraffes helped the elephant in this enchanting story, and now you can find them traveling in the parade on the rooftop.

☐ Find Dr. Seuss at the parade

In another scene from *And to Think I Saw it on Mulberry Street,* next door to Mulberry Street™ Store, you will see the policeman going past the judges. Be sure to hop aboard the second motorcycle and get a sweet picture in this area.

If you look at the judges, you will notice one has a beard and glasses. This character was inspired by none other than Dr. Seuss himself.

- [ ] Read the story of the Sneetches in the queue for the High in the Sky Seuss Trolley Train Ride

    Read about the Sneetches with stars and the Sneetches without as you wind your way through the queue for the High in the Sky Seuss Trolley Train Ride. This classic tale by Dr. Seuss teaches about tolerance and acceptance in a whimsical child-friendly way, and now you can relive this tale during a short time before your ride.

- [ ] Ride the High in the Sky Seuss Trolley Train Ride

    Ride high above the streets of Seuss Landing™ as you board this colorful trolley. You have the chance to ride one of two different tracks to either see the story of the Sneetches or take a complete tour of Seuss Landing.

    This fun trolley gives you a great view of the attractions and Circus McGurkus before you arrive back at the train station to complete your ride.

☐ Get ice cream at Hop on Pop

> Step up to the Hop on Pop ice cream stand and get a cold sundae on a stick or a waffle cone heaping with your favorite ice cream flavors. These delectable ice cream items offer a cold treat on a hot day, so step up and get your favorite at Hop on Pop.

☐ Find the Zax Bypass

> As you explore Seuss Landing, you can walk towards the water and find the Zax Bypass. These two stubborn Zax will not move out of the way as they are stuck in this never-ending impasse.
>
> This area holds another secret little known at Universal's Islands of Adventure. The Zax Bypass is the spot where the groundbreaking of Universal's Islands of Adventure took place, and this cute Dr. Seuss reference marks the spot.

☐ Get a picture with the Cat in the Hat

> Guests of Seuss Landing may come face to face with the most famous cat in all of the children's literature, the Cat in the Hat. This favorite literary character is waiting for you to pose for pictures and sign autographs near his namesake ride, so keep an eye out for the Cat in the Hat.

☐ Get a picture with the Grinch

> The villain that lives on Mount Crumpit comes to Seuss Landing to pose for pictures and torment guests who cross his path. See if you can get the Grinch to behave long enough to get some fun pictures before he disappears to his mountain once again.

☐ Get a picture with Thing 1 and Thing 2

> Thing 1 and Thing 2, those pesky friends of the Cat in the Hat can be found in Seuss Landing, getting into trouble and posing for pictures with the guests of Seuss Landing.
>
> Try to capture these two scamps and get some creative pictures.

☐ See a performance of, Oh! The Stories You'll Hear!

> Join the residents of Seuss Landing in a musical telling of your favorite Dr. Seuss stories. Performed on the streets of Seuss Landing, you can clap along with the songs as the characters dance and sing to the stories made famous throughout the years.
>
> Be sure to make time for this show for the entire family.

☐ Read a story at the All the Books You Can Read shop

> Step into the All the Books You Can Read shop in Seuss Landing, where the whole world is at your feet when you open a new book. The stories inside the books can take your little ones on adventures with new friends, so be sure to spend some time in this shop and bring home these classic books as souvenirs.

☐ Walk through the Truffula trees

> As you explore Seuss Landing, you will come to a forest that has been mostly cut down. Only a few of the Truffula trees remain for you to explore, and the Lorax is standing nearby to keep them safe.

☐ Listen to the pipes of the Once-ler's House

> Step up to the Once-ler's huge house and listen to the pipes to hear the story of the Lorax and the last of the Truffula Trees that are growing because of caring people who planted the last seeds of these rare trees.

☐ Ride the Caro-Seuss-el™

> Select your character from the fifty-six animals and get ready for a crazy ride. Hold on to the reins and make your animal move as you ride up

and down. These adorable animals offer a fun new ride on the traditional carousel, so do not miss this creative ride.

☐ Find the twisted palm trees

If you look at the enormous palm trees in the Seuss Landing™ area, you will notice that they grow in the same twisted patterns as the building throughout this area. This was not a design but a result of Hurricane Andrew in 1992.

The hurricane winds caused the bends, and Universal's Islands of Adventure decided they would be perfect in this area of the theme park.

☐ Visit Circus McGurkus Café Stoo-pendus

Step inside Circus McGurkus Café Stoo-pendus and enjoy a great meal while reliving this adorable children's book. The acrobats are high overhead while guests eat within the train cars that encircle the café.

See the circus organ that plays whimsical music for the performers and look out for the Seuss High in the Sky Trolley that comes through the big top.

The Cat in the Hat™

☐ Get your picture with the Cat in the Hat™ sign

> Outside the Cat in the Hat™, you will find an incredibly large sign with the household items balancing precariously on top.
>
> The huge hat is the great photo op for guests looking for a cute picture within Seuss Landing™.

☐ Read the story of the Cat in the Hat in the queue

> The story of the Cat in the Hat™ begins before you step into your ride vehicle. If you watch the walls as you walk through the queue, you will see the story appear and fade from the walls of the queue.
>
> Keep an eye out for this classic story as you enter the Cat in the Hat™.

☐ Visit the Cat in the Hat™

> Step into your couch and set off through the story of the Cat in the Hat™. Join Sally and Conrad as you watch the Cat attempt to play during a rainy day with Thing 1 and Thing 2. Watch as their pet fish tries to stop the destruction before mother gets home.

Wander through the house and finally watch as the Cat cleans up the mess just in time.

☐ Visit the Cats, Hats and Things store

As you exit your ride with the Cat in the Hat, you will come to the Cats, Hats, and Things store where you can find your favorite Cat and the Hat themed merchandise.

Inside, you will find everything from clothing, plush toys, and books with characters from the beloved children's book, so spend some time exploring the Cats, Hats, and Things Store.

☐ Walk through If I Ran a Zoo

Walk through the crazy zoo with twists and turns where you find yourself face to face with the strangest animals you will ever see.

Explore this interactive zoo as you push buttons, turn levels, ride the animals, and look through the hedges throughout. Be careful, or you will find yourself getting wet along the way.

☐ Ride One Fish Two Fish Red Fish Blue Fish™

Hop aboard a fish and ride with One Fish Two Fish Red Fish Blue Fish™ as you circle the pond. Fly your fish up and down along the way, but be careful of the water effects that will spray you on your ride.

☐ Explore McElligot's Pool

Near the One Fish Two Fish Red Fish Blue Fish™ attraction, you will find McElligot's Pool. This small pool is stocked with the imaginary fish from this classic children's story. Look around to read the signs to tell the story of McElligot and his pool.

☐ Find the nest with Horton's eggs

Hidden within Seuss Landing™ is the small nest with the red egg sat on by Horton. Now you can sit atop this brightly colored egg for a great photo opportunity.

Look for the Horton eggs behind the Cats, Hats, and Things Store.

☐ Try a treat from Green Eggs and Ham

Just behind the Caro-Seuss-sel, you will find the massive green ham and green egg umbrellas. Green Eggs and Ham offers tater tots with great toppings, including the signature green eggs and ham.

Stop by to try this treat as you spend time in Seuss Landing™.

In conclusion, I hope you have enjoyed seeing the Universal Orlando resort with *One Hundred Things to do at Universal Orlando Before you Die*. It has been my great pleasure writing this book, and I hope you have found something that has added to your enjoyment during your time in the theme parks.

I look forward to too many years of the Universal Orlando resort growing and changing. These theme parks have been a part of my life since I was a small child, and I look forward to many more.

www.ingramcontent.com/pod-product-compliance
Lightning Source LLC
Chambersburg PA
CBHW071344080526
44587CB00017B/2952